Nasione R. Silva Rodrigues Silva

The aesthetics of memory and confession in Maria Moura's memoir

Nasione R. Silva Rodrigues Silva

The aesthetics of memory and confession in Maria Moura's memoir

From memory to confession

Imprint
Any brand names and product names mentioned in this book are subject to trademark, brand or patent protection and are trademarks or registered trademarks of their respective holders. The use of brand names, product names, common names, trade names, product descriptions etc. even without a particular marking in this work is in no way to be construed to mean that such names may be regarded as unrestricted in respect of trademark and brand protection legislation and could thus be used by anyone.

Cover image: Provided by the author

This book is a translation from the original published under ISBN 978-613-9-72951-7.

Publisher:
Sciencia Scripts
is a trademark of
Dodo Books Indian Ocean Ltd. and OmniScriptum S.R.L publishing group

120 High Road, East Finchley, London, N2 9ED, United Kingdom
Str. Armeneasca 28/1, office 1, Chisinau MD-2012, Republic of Moldova, Europe
Printed at: see last page
ISBN: 978-620-7-75111-2

I dedicate this work *in memoriam to* my parents: Antonio Rodrigues Galvão and Maria do Bonfim Rodrigues Gama, for having been my examples in life, because they always told me that it is in studying that we acquire knowledge. As they always said, "no one can take knowledge away from us", and I carry this with me with the certainty that acquired values are to be valued and passed on, when they are for the common good.

I dedicate this immensely to my beloved sons Luis Antonio and Arthur Ávila, for their encouragement and especially to my husband Airton, for his patience with my absence due to the hours I spent studying.

I thank God in the first place and Mary Most Holy, because with the spiritual strength I believe I have received, I have been able to complete this project.

I would like to thank my supervisor, Professor Walnice Aparecida Matos Vilalva, who, with her wisdom and patience, was able to understand my anxieties and guide me along the paths to be followed in our research. And to all the professors at PPGEL-UNEMAT, who knew how to conduct their classes with wisdom.

To Capes, which provided me with the grant to carry out this research.

To all my classmates, thank you very much.

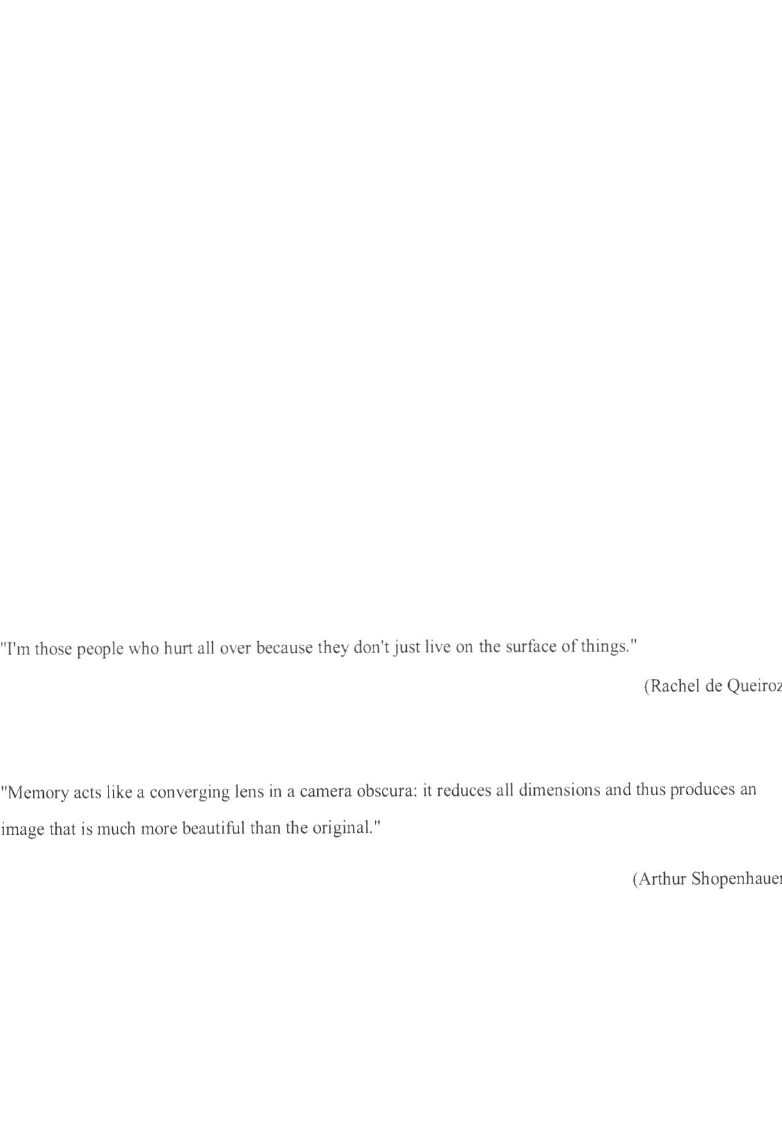

"I'm those people who hurt all over because they don't just live on the surface of things."

(Rachel de Queiroz)

"Memory acts like a converging lens in a camera obscura: it reduces all dimensions and thus produces an image that is much more beautiful than the original."

(Arthur Shopenhauer)

ABSTRACT: The aim of this work is to study the configuration of memory and confession in the discourse of the character Maria Moura in Rachel de Queiroz's **Memorial** de **Maria Moura** (2000). We analyse the memorial discourse as transgressive. The narrative of the "I", which brings out the strength of the female character in a patriarchal society, portrays a complex awareness of the world and of herself. As theoretical support, we highlight Bakhtin in The **Aesthetics of Verbal Creation** (2006); and **Questions of Literature and Aesthetics - The Theory of the Novel** (2010), Henri Bergson (2011) in **Matter and Memory.**

Keywords: Literature, Discourse, Memory, Rachel de Queiroz.

SUMMARY

INTRODUCTION

When I read Rachel de Queiroz for the first time, I was impressed. Perhaps because of my immaturity. No, it wasn't immaturity. I realised that in this author's writing, in the way she approaches memory and the discourse of characters in marginalised areas, the human question is re-signified on an aesthetic level, giving dimension to the sertão. In this sense, Rachel de Queiroz is part of a generation of Brazilian writers who, with encouragement, denounce human misery as it is truly experienced.

Rachel presents us with female characters who are always on the move, in search of new horizons, who surprise us with their petty, selfish and contradictory feelings. They are idealists, mothers, daughters, harlots and saints. In life, they lead a life of conflict, of struggle, with causes to defend. In this sense, they are affirmative and have a profound social sense. In her article Ethos de Rachel[1] , Heloísa Buarque de Hollanda states:

> In Rachel's stories, on the other hand, the deeds, daring and daily life of the ladies of the sertão shone through. Her narrative, while betraying a certain pride, brought to the present, above all, the memory of the various forms of female power that have been forgotten and/or destroyed throughout history. I realised that to study women in Brazil and in Brazilian literature without going through Rachel de Queiroz is, to say the least, imprudent.

We certainly agree with what Hollanda argues, because in Rachel's works we find Marias, Marialvas, Beatas, Conceição, all marked by a deep sense of justice.

Rachel de Queiroz was born on 17 November 1910 in Fortaleza. She became an extraordinary journalist, chronicler and novelist who, on publishing her first novel, O **Quinze** (1930), caused astonishment and admiration among one of the great authors of that time, as stated in **Caderno de Literatura brasileira,** organised by Franceschi (1997, p.16), in which Graciliano Ramos, on reading Rachel's work, says: "she's a man", later Graciliano himself admits. "For a long time, I had the idea that she was a man, so strong was the prejudice in me that excluded women from literature." Recognition also came from Manuel Bandeira, who dedicated a poem to her, calling her the 'cream and flower of our people' 'and praised her love as an aunt'. Calos Heitor Cony refers to Rachel saying: "I have always admired in her the woman who is courageous in her views, capable of attitudes that almost never please the fads of intellectual life. An obstinate northeasterner, you can always expect from her the firmness of her convictions and the tenderness of her generosity." (FRANCESCHI, 1997, p.16). Nelly Novais Coelho adds that with the publication of this work (O Quinze) the repercussion was immediate in the literary world and several authors also recognised it, such as:

> Augusto Frederico Schmidt, Artur Mota, Mário de Andrade, Agripino Grieco, Gastão Cruls, Antonio Sales, Beni de Carvalho and others from various states greeted the book with the enthusiasm of those discovering a work of authentic value. And the unknown young woman from Ceará, from one moment to the next, was honoured nationally with the Graça Aranha Prize from the Brazilian Academy of Letters, and hailed as the first great female voice of Modernism, in the field of the novel. (COELHO, 2002, p.552).

Mário de Andrade adds to Rachel:

> Rarely have I come across prose in our language that is more... prosystic, if I may put it that way. The rhythm is of an admirable elasticity, very serene, rich in the dispersion of stresses, without those short periodicities of accents that are so detrimental to prose, metrifying it, giving it oratorical or poetic movement. The sentences move in light, comfortable breaths, varied with magnificent skill. Perhaps there is no one in Brazil now who writes the national language with the limpid beauty that Rachel de Queiroz gives it. I'm merely extolling the exceptional clarity of this daughter of the Ceará moonlight, (apud. HOLLANDA, 2004, p.7)

Not surprisingly, Rachel was less than 20 years old when she published her first novel; for Heloisa Buarque de Hollanda, Rachel "is considered one of the most important Brazilian writers of the 20th century." (HOLLANDA, 2004, p.7). She is the author of seven novels, all of which have been critically acclaimed. Her works have a regionalist authenticity that consolidated her as a female figure in Brazilian literature, as well as the female figure in the literary universe with the character Conceição in **O Quinze.** When we talk about regionalist authenticity, it's because Rachel was part of a literary movement that had its mark on the northeastern hinterland in the 1930s. We won't be working on Regionalism in our research.

Prior to the publication of **O Quinze,** the novelist worked as a journalist, "and a journalist is what she liked to be", as we can see in Rachel's argument, "First of all, I'm a journalist." (HOLLANDA, 2004, p.7).

When she is crowned queen of the students in the governor's office, she learns of João Pessoa's death. Rachel throws her crown on the floor and rushes out, saying: "I'm a reporter". Here we see a woman with a strong personality and a competent professional. With the publication of **João Miguel** (1932), Rachel breaks with the Communist Party, because her "comrades" don't accept what is written in the book, as Rachel herself tells us:

> The president, declaring that he had just arrived from the Soviet Union (they never said Russia), had express orders to curb intellectual offences. He said he had read

> my novel carefully (...). If you don't make the basic changes, we can't publish your novel. He held in his hands, on a roll of brown paper, the only copy of the book I had, barely typed by myself (...). I slowly got up from my seat. I approached the table, held out my hand and asked for the originals so that I could make the required changes. The stern man handed over the roll. I looked back and saw that the shed door was open, its only exit. And instead of going back to the bench, I walked to the middle of the room, turned to the table and said in a loud, calm voice: "I don't recognise in my companions the literary conditions to give an opinion on my work. I'm not going to make any corrections. And good riddance!" (QUEIROZ, R. QUEIROZ, M. Luizade. 2004, p.48-49).

In 1937 he published **Caminhos de Pedras.** With the advent of the Estado Novo Decree, copies of her novel were burnt. She was detained for three months in the cinema room of the fire brigade in Fortaleza on charges of subversion. According to COELHO (2002), this was because Rachel de Queiroz had. "A spirit attentive to political and social problems, she disagreed with the direction of politics in the 1930s (the end of the Old Republic). (...)" (COELHO, 2002, p.551). We can see that Rachel had clarity when producing her works, she wasn't afraid to denounce the ills that the less favoured, or even those with whom she disagreed, were denounced, which in a way caused her personal inconvenience, because she wasn't understood by those who felt offended.

We believe that both the novels **João Miguel** (1932) and **Caminhos** de **Pedras** (1937), although they are not the subject of our research, are worth mentioning because they are works that also made Raquel de Queiroz stand out in Brazilian literature, as they are works of great relevance in the literary critical process of a social context.

From being a contributor to **Correio da Manhã** and **O Jornal** and **Diário da Tarde,** Rachel went on to become an exclusive columnist for **O Cruzeiro** magazine for a long time. She also worked as a translator of *"best sellers of* universal literature in English, French and Spanish (Emily Brontë, Jane Austen, Dostievski, Tolstoy, Balzac, St Teresa of Avila and others)". (COELHO, 2002, p.551).

Rachel found herself drawn to the theatre and wrote two plays: one in 1953, **Lampião,** which was staged at the Municipal Theatre in Rio de Janeiro and at the Leopoldo Fróes Theatre in São Paulo, and was considered the best play of the year and was awarded the Saci Prize; the second, **A beata Maria do Egito** was published in 1958; this play was performed at the National Comedy Theatre, at the Serrador Theatre in Rio de Janeiro, which won her the INL, Paula Brito and Roberto Gomes/Federal District Prizes. In **A beata Maria do Egito** we see the fragmentation of the subject, the human frustration impregnated in the being, the search for fulfilment, for an ideology in the midst of so much social folly.

Forty-five years after the publication of her first novel, Rachel published **Dôra Doralina** (1975). It features a character (Dôra) who tries to assume her own freedom, but who suffers from the indifference of her mother in particular. In this sense, Nelly Novais Coelho (2002) observes of the characters that "they are all dramatic figures of enormous human grandeur, but defrauded as lovers, mothers or daughters, by a kind of predestination. Frustrated as mothers, most of Rachel's female characters are frustrated as daughters." (COELHO, 2002, p.552).

In **Memorial de Maria Moura** (1992), Rachel presents us with the character Maria Moura as an individual who searches her soul for knowledge of herself, as the truth to change her world. Drawing inferences from Coelho (2002), we realise that:

> (...) this populated loneliness, ancient loneliness, running in the blood, loneliness mixed with an inordinate feeling of communion and power over the world and men, which we see emerging twelve years after Dôra, in the personality of Maria Moura, one of the most fascinating characters in the Brazilian novel of yesterday and today (COELHO, 2002, p.553).

So we have a character who makes us rethink the reality of being in a constant search for transformation. In her we see the manifestation of consciousness as a phenomenon of representation of the subject in the face of their condition in the world. Ligia Chiapinni (2002), quoting Gilberto Freyre, says that the author's work leads us to discuss and, at the same time, observe that Rachel de Queiroz, by introducing female characters, "to the extent that her heroines leave the womb, the region and the big house to take to the streets, and more than the streets, to the road, arriving at boarding houses in the cities, schools, reading, studying and freely choosing their partners and professions" (CHIAPPINI, 2002, p.175), proves the break with the Pernambuco sociologist's regional and national proposal. In this sense, we can say that Rachel de Queiroz is mature as a novelist, with a revolutionary spirit and liberal sentiment, capable of bringing about transformations in a world of inhuman exploitation and social injustice.

Memorial de Maria Moura, according to Coelho (2002), is Rachel's "summit novel", because the work is "touched by the post-modern winds", in other words, a work that reinvents its origins and "reveals itself as a complex amalgam of reality/invention, history/myth, sacred/profane". (COELHO, 2002, p.553). We can't deny that in **Memorial de Maria Moura,** the character Maria Moura has an inner perspective, with her memory moulded into existential roots that nourish her in order to deal with the mismatches of the world in which she finds herself.

In her works, Rachel de Queiroz brings underlying sentiments of high values, in favour of reflecting on social and political realities. In this sense, the novelist received several honours, but the most important of all was the recognition by the Brazilian Academy of Letters, where Rachel de Queiroz became the first woman to hold a chair, number 5, in 1977.

This work focuses on the study of the configuration of memory, through the lens of discourse in **Memorial de Maria Moura** (1992), more specifically, from the *Configuration of memory and confession in Maria Moura's discourse.* Memory comes into perspective in this approach because it is one of the greatest resources in Rachel de Queiroz's work. It is through memory that the discourses of the female characters establish ideological relationships, feeding on the past and reinventing themselves in the present.

In the first chapter, we focus on the role of the female character in Rachel de Queiroz's novel, considering the construction of Conceição in **O Quinze** (1930), passing through Dôra in **Dôra Doralina (1975);** the Beata, from **A beata Maria do Egito (1958),** and Marialva, from **Memorial de Maria Moura** (1992), focussing on discourse, memory and identity, between the ideals of freedom and tradition.

In the second chapter, we work on memory, situating its configuration in Maria Moura's free direct discourse, the ideological discourse: the conquest of land, respect and power. And in the last chapter, we look at the conformation of confession, how memory becomes confession, according to the assumption of sincerity.

1. THE FEMALE CHARACTER IN

NOVEL BY RACHEL DE QUEIROZ

Brazilian literature in the late 19th and early 20th centuries was marked by regional novels. Amongst the many writers who became involved in this trend, Rachel de Queiroz stands out with her works **O Quinze** (1930) and **João Miguel** (1932), both of which are set in Ceará. Bosi (2006) considers that the author anticipated the great emphasis that the narratives would have on the social themes of the northeast.

For Nelly Novais Coelho (2002), in **O Quinze** Rachel de Queiroz presents language as,

> (...) verbal artlessness, his seething words, his emotional restraint and lack of sentimentality were, immediately, the elements that made the denunciations contained in his fabulation more forceful: the tragic exploitation of man by man (aggravated by the clemency of nature) and that of the prejudices cobbled together in patriarchal society, especially those that subordinated women to men, imprisoning them in the duality of reciprocally exclusive faces (queen of the home or mistress) and preventing their freedom of choice and action, within their environment or the nation. This double problem is experienced by Conceição in this first novel (COELHO, 2002, p. 552).

In this sense, we have Rachel de Queiroz's critically focussed curtailment of the right to freedom of thought, action and love, which until then had been denied to women. **O Quinze** is undoubtedly a landmark work in Rachel de Queiroz's literary production, as it is her first novel, and it also marks the writer's insertion into Brazilian literature.

The plot of the novel presents two distinct planes: the saga of the retreatants fleeing the drought in the north-east, and an (imaginary) love affair, focussed on Conceição's perception. The narrative develops in the apparently informal voice of the heterodiegetic narrator, who has knowledge of the story being told and the universe of the characters. In the space of the sertão, the narrative presents the universe of the northeast (Ceará) and chronological time, although not exclusively. However, in Conceição we can perceive the enchantment of memory, because its aesthetic unity is constituted by the timeline from childhood to adulthood. It can be said that the same narrator narrates from two different perspectives: the story of the retirantes and the story of Conceição. There are therefore two parallel narratives that make up the novelistic aesthetic in **O Quinze.**

In Chico Bento's narrative, we are taken on the journey of the northeastern retreatants, we learn about the family nucleus of the character, a man from the sertão, a cowboy, married and the father of five children. His wife Cordolina, who used to be fat, is now, after the drought, "as thin as death". In this image of Chico Bento's wife, we see that the social portrait of misery is highlighted by the (un)human condition, problematised from the perspective of the condition of the retreatant, resulting in hunger and death. With the onset of drought, Chico Bento decides to go north to work with rubber. On the way, one of his sons dies of poisoning. After burying his son by the side of the road, the family continues their journey with deep bitterness and suffering.

In Conceição's narrative, we meet the motherless girl who was brought up by her grandmother, a wealthy lady. As a child, Conceição acquires a taste for reading. She reads several books and becomes a teacher. Her profession and reading endow her with otherness, a cultured character with elevated feelings, bathed in deep humanity. Her love partner, Vicente, is a rough man, a cattle farmer and a cousin in love. However, the courtship doesn't happen because of the differences between the two. With the drought, Conceição's family temporarily moves from the farm to the city; with the end of the drought, her grandmother returns to Logradouro, but Conceição decides to stay in the city, taking responsibility for her own life, which for the time was not accepted by society.

We can say that **O Quinze** is a work that expresses the barbarity and torment of the retirantes. But in the face of so much suffering, the narrator introduces us to the character Conceição, who brings with her a deep sense of humanity and affection. Conceição is a character who masterfully straddles both planes of the narrative. Through her, we realise the clash of realities, the encounters and mismatches amidst the suffering caused by drought and poverty.

Throughout the plot, we realise that Conceição differs from the other characters in that she is aware of her actions. By helping Chico Bento in his quest for better days, she is helping herself. In this way, we see Conceição, the novel's protagonist, with her experience and feelings, the border between the miserable and the rich. According to Bakhtin (2006, p.91), the character is aware of what she wants and that through her speech, or her words, she tells herself and expresses her point of view in a series of events. In this sense, the character is searching for their ideal life, they recognise themselves as being able to take control of their life and their ideals.

As we've already pointed out, Conceição is a character who likes to read and has feminist tendencies, due to the world of reading she acquired as a child, living with her grandmother in Logradouro. "Those books - a hundred at the most - were old companions that she chose at random, to savour a piece here, another there, another there, in the course of the evening." (QUEIROZ, 1930, p.12). This intellectual world in which Conceição is inserted makes her different, because she considers herself free and able to stand on her own; unlike Dôra who insists on maintaining the family. "Conceição was twenty-two and didn't talk about getting married. Her few attempts at dating had gone with her eighteen years and her time as a normalista; she happily said that she was born a spinster." (QUEIROZ, 1930, p.13). With this conviction that she was capable of living on her own, she breaks with values and customs, doesn't marry, has her own profession and salary, and dedicates herself to social causes.

In this sense, the aesthetic realisation is developed in the narrative from a social and psychological perspective, centred on the character Conceição, who questions her destiny and her truths, because "accustomed to thinking for herself, to living in isolation, she had created her own ideas and prejudices, sometimes broad, sometimes bold, and which were sinned against mainly by the excessiveness of the house." (QUEIROZ, 1930, p.14).

Between her courtship and marriage to Vicente, Conceição's trajectory in the novel, as a plane of intimacy, indicates a barrier that rises as the character asserts herself as a conscience and freedom:

> Vicente listened to her with distant thoughts, displeased by the indifferent and didactic tone in which the girl spoke (...). When I left, I was overwhelmed by a vague but oppressive feeling of disgust. Because Conceição was so distant and distracted... (...). Lying in bed with the light off, Conceição remembered Vicente and his visit (...). He was good to listen to and to look at, like a beautiful landscape whose only requirement was beauty and colour. (...). She thought that even the powerful charm that his healthy fortitude exerted on her would not fulfil the tremendous width that separated them. (QUEIROZ, 1930, p.80-82).

Unlike Dôra, who seems to be opting for freedom, but prefers to return to the submissive condition of marriage, to her birthplace, to her past, her childhood, adolescence and wifely environment, the cycle of a lifetime in a single home, the birthplace that cancels out the possibility of the oneiric home. The superimposition of the natal home onto the oneiric home allows for Dôra's conservative human conscience, and her commitment to the reproduction of consolidated values, her unity, therefore, is conformative and affirmative.

Forty years after her first publication, amid countless chronicles, Rachel de Queiroz came up with the novel **Dôra Doralina** (1975), with a profile that broke with some of the social paradigms of the 70s. The novel is divided into three parts: the first, "The Lady's Book"; the second, "The Company's Book" and the third, "The Commander's Book". It is as a memoir that Rachel de Queiroz problematises the condition of women in the face of the values imposed by patriarchal society.

Our understanding of memory is based on H. Bergson's concept in **Matter and Memory** (2011). Although the theorist classifies two types of memory that we could summarise as collective and individual, our analysis highlights the involuntary type of memory-remembrance, motivated by perceptions in the present.

In the first part of the novel, "The Book of Senhora", the narrator-character introduces us to her mother, Senhora, as she calls her, a determined and domineering woman who takes over men's space in the sertão. Dôra, for her part, feels that she is not welcome in her own home, that she doesn't have her mother's love and that she suffers from the absence of the father she lost as a child. Her mother seems to be jealous of her daughter's youth. The daughter grows up and marries Laurindo. The unhappy marriage produces a son who is never born. From the family made up of mother, daughter and son-in-law, the main conflict of the narrative is born: the love triangle between mother, daughter and son-in-law, generating a dispute, dislike and breaking the bonds of affection and love.

Dôra, having been widowed, finds in this event the way to acquire her freedom. She moves from the Soledade farm to Fortaleza, from the backlands to the city. There, she works as an administrator in a boarding house. In the second part, "O Livro da Companhia", the character meets and becomes part of a theatre company. She becomes an actress. She meets a captain. Together with the company, she moves to Rio de Janeiro. In the capital, the captain rents a house where they live together. The third part, "O Livro do Comandante" (The Commander's Book), shows Dôra's life in this new marriage. After some time, she receives news of her mother's death and, with the death of her second husband, Dôra returns to the Soledade farm.

"WELL, AS THE COMMANDER SAID, it always hurts. It only doesn't hurt once you're dead, because life is an eternal ache." (QUEIROZ, 2004, p.13) Based on this fragment, we can see how the character narrates what his life was like, the awareness he expresses of suffering and loneliness. It's important to note that, as far as the character's memory is concerned, these paths are marked more by feelings of sadness, as she herself says when she recounts her dream of having a daughter to give her the name "Alegria" (Joy), because joy should remain alive with "vivid colours", while the bad should be erased as a "bad thing".

All the expectations and frustrations of the character Dôra are presented by this autodiegetic narrator[2], who becomes a character in her own right; memory gives rise to the writing of the self. "I shrugged my shoulders. At that time, what did I care about the language of the people? (...). Since I was a little girl, I had been preparing myself, building up the courage for that adventure." (QUEIROZ, 2004, p.109,113).

We notice that it is through free direct speech that the character reflects, in sadness, on what life, error and deceit are. "That's the mistake, nobody wants to accept the replacements; we welcome the new ones and even like them, but without giving up the old ones. And that can't happen, how would the world look?" (QUEIROZ, 2004, p.15). In this form of discourse, Authier Revuz (2004, p.12) announces that only the single speaker produces a thread of discourse in which the other is inscribed. It is the other of the discourse reported by the syntactic forms of indirect or free direct discourse. In this case of a memorial discourse, it is the other of oneself, separated by time, reunited in the act of memory, integrating present and past on the level of enunciation.

In this configuration of memory, we realise the psychological density of the character Dôra, the way in which she feeds on her memory-remembrance that brings back the experience, in the form of feeling and perception of herself and the other. The other is the Mother she no longer calls Mother, but Lady. In this narrative journey, we realise the strength of mother and daughter, the way they both stand up to the social and family context. The daughter asks why she is called Maria das Dores. Her mother explains that it's because of a promise she made at the time of her birth. "- The name was a promise, I've said it so many times. I made a promise to Our Lady of Sorrows so that I wouldn't die in childbirth. I don't know if you know, but it almost killed me." (QUEIROZ, 2004, p.30). Dôra suspects that her mother must blame her for almost dying. Her daughter's conscience is made by her mistrust of her mother. She wonders why her mother never answers her

---

[2] See (REIS; LOPES. 1988 p. 118)

questions about her father. What she knows about the father figure are the little fragments told to her by Xavinha, the maid who had a special affection for Dôra, an affection that Dôra wished she had received from her mother. It is through the stories told by the maid that Dôra is born with the idealised father image.

Throughout the first part of the novel, the insistent questions search for an identity from their childhood, for the origin of the name Maria das Dores, "- I hate it, but I hate my name and all its nicknames: Maria das Dores, Dôra, Dasdores, Dôrinha, Dôrita". (QUEIROZ, 2004, p.30), pain that would separate them for life. The unsatisfactory answers that lead to conflict between mother and daughter: this is the theme of the novel. And this makes this novel unique in Brazilian literature, as it is possibly the only one that deals with female representation in the conflict between mother and daughter.

A sense of conflict that escalates to the point of expressing the daughter's hatred for her mother. This hatred is caused by a lack of affection and rivalry. Let's take a look at the daughter's description in the narrative: "With Madam, it had always seemed to me since I was a little girl that I had to fight even about sleeping hours; (...). When I was a little girl, she always sent someone to wash me, dress me and comb my smooth tresses." (QUEIROZ, 2004, p.47). On the other hand, we see in the character Senhora, the mother, a strong, solitary woman who makes decisions according to her own determination. Everyone respects her and Dôra, despite her hatred, describes her with traits of beauty and strength.

> She was so pretty and rosy, barely over forty, her beautiful blonde hair half falling apart in a bun of tortoiseshell hairpins, her short-sleeved linen dress revealing her round arms, her cleavage open, her bosom soft. (...)? - She'd come to the table smelling fresh and flushed, sometimes even with her hair down, in frilly kimonos that dragged on the floor (...), she'd put on flat shoes and her white linen dresses (...) (QUEIROZ, 2004, p.25,27).

But as Senhora was a domineering woman who had control over everyone and everything, Dôra says.

> (...) in that house in Soledade I never really felt like an owner, more like a guest who had nothing of my own (...). In fact, nobody on the farm said Senhora anymore - only "the owner". "A dona quer", "a donamandou". (QUEIROZ, 2004, p. 47).

From physical differences to differences in relationships and affection, the narrative profiles the affection that characterises the relationship between these female characters, mother and daughter. In the conception of the traditional family, the patriarchal system, a role is expected of the woman - mother, housewife - whose chores should be to look after the children and her husband. The mother should find in the image of her daughter her reflection of values and principles. However, Rachel de Queiroz knew how to present these characters in a way that problematised these family horizons, their consolidated roles, especially motherhood as a synonym for unconditional love.

In the open proposal to retrace the past, the narrator-character's discourse is constituted by a memorialised account, which moves from childhood to adulthood, in the search for the totality of life, in the anguish of what has been lived. "If the girl I was more than twenty years ago and the record has registered, today she is lost, buried in time, just like death - yes, (...)." (QUEIROZ, 2004, p.412). And in this unravelling of the thread of memory, one can see the flow of life, life being wiped clean, suffering and pain.

From her childhood conflict, from the absence of maternal love, the narrator is faced with a new phase in their relationship: participation in the love triangle. The book is made up of a triad: the first, second and third chapters, the love triangle between mother, daughter and son-in-law. This shows the audacity of the narrative in a patriarchal social context, while at the same time breaking the paradigms of motherhood and its established values.

The love triangle is formed by Laurindo, an ambitious surveyor who arrives at the Soledade farm to measure land boundaries and sees it as a safe harbour. He seduces Dôra and they marry. However, there is no joy to be found in this marriage, Dôra becomes pregnant but loses her child, as we mentioned earlier *"... life is an eternal ache"*. In order to talk about her mother's betrayal of her husband, the protagonist-narrator recalls the arrival of Raimundo Delmiro on the Soledade farm, who, having been treated ill by Dôra, began to live on the farm in a "tapera" house, even against Senhora's wishes. Delmiro thanked Dôra and became her great admirer and friend. And one night when Delmiro, as was his custom, brought something to Dôra to exchange for other food, the two met and talked quietly so as not to be noticed inside the house, but to their surprise, they heard a noise coming from Senhora's room. This is confirmation of the betrayal.

> (...) when suddenly there was a muffled sound, the sound of a voice, in the room opposite - which was the Lady's room, next to the living room.
> And I heard her speak (I'd never been able to speak quietly in my life), yes it was hers:
> - Go away!
> And then Laurindo's voice, protesting: (...) (QUEIROZ, 2004, p.92).
> Dôra despairs, runs, cries and Delmiro asks her to go into the house because it's "cold". As she leaves, she says: "God will find a way". I raised my face at that word and said my words too: - Only death will do." (QUEIROZ, 2004, p.92)

The love triangle, once discovered, is soon undone by the mysterious death of her husband Laurindo. The narrative raises the possibility of Dôra's revenge. The enigma is not unravelled. With Laurindo's death, the character seeks new horizons and the desire for freedom manifests itself in "skin" and "living flesh", calling for the desire of the "I" as a safe alternative for a new life. The transformation is seen in the second part of the novel: from housewife to actress, Dôra receives a new name and ventures out and about in a theatre company.

> I took off my mourning for the journey. If I could, I'd take off my skin, pull out my hair, come out in living flesh (...). I closed my mouth tightly, I didn't answer, but I didn't change my clothes. I crossed the whole of Aroeiras, bought a ticket, waited,

took the train, dressed in blue (QUEIROZ, 2004, p.109).

This transition between worlds, heralding a new perspective for the character, is symbolically expressed by the blue dress... *"dressed in blue"?* The Dictionary of Symbols characterises the colour blue as:

> Blue is the **deepest** of colours: in it, the gaze plunges without encountering any obstacle, losing itself to infinity, as if in a perpetual fugue of colour. (...) blue dematerialises everything that is impregnated by it. Blue is the colour of infinity, where the real is transformed into the imaginary. (CHEVALIER. GHEERBRANT. 1998, p. 106-107).

The family is torn apart with the death of her husband and the abandonment of her home and mother, or even her birthplace. This causes a rupture in the protagonist's perspective in the narrative and her trajectory takes a different turn: she leaves the countryside, her home environment, and goes to the city; from married to widowed; from housewife to actress. In this sense, according to Bakhtin (2006, p.173-174), the narrator takes on a new reality, a different way of living, because before she had someone to do everything for her, now she doesn't. With her freedom and her profession, this character is affirming her new life ideals.

We notice that Dôra's desire for freedom is, in a way, acquired from the moment she leaves the farm, and the narrative characterises her in a new space, the urban one. Work guarantees her livelihood, while at the same time imprinting the new profile of the woman who was born in the 70s of the 20th century. Turned to work as a desire and a choice, Dôra can't forget her past, her home and her mother.

> Little did she know that my leaving home hadn't been a passing heartbreak. That I had cut the cord that tied me to Soledade forever and never again. From Soledade and her owner, all I wanted now was the distance and the few memories (QUEIROZ, 2004, p. 121).

In Dôra, she anticipates and signals the profound transformation of women in the 20th century, launching an understanding of the perception of the future. The narrative overcomes the private nature of the experience, of the search for freedom, it becomes mature and believes that it can be free and follow its own path, it creates and affiliates itself to a greater extent with history. As Bakhtin infers:

> Man was forming, developing, changing the scope of his time (...). Man was being formed and not the world itself: the world, on the other hand, was an immovable point of reference for the developing man (...). This is precisely the formation of the new man; therefore, the organising force of the future is immense here, and of course we are not talking about the future in private-biographical terms, but in historical terms. (...). Here the image of man in formation begins to overcome its private character (up to a point, of course) and ends up in another *vast* sphere, and in everything it is different from historical existence. (BAKHTIN, 2006, pp. 221-

222).

Freedom and financial independence are the second phase of the character's life: the profession of actress had brought them to her. She was given the name Nely Sorel. In this new phase, the character takes on an audacious shape and profile for the time. In her new world, Dora creates her own domain, acquires freedom, is recognised and applauded. But this condition doesn't erase the past or even diminish the marks and remnants of time. In this awareness, the character discovers that changing her name from Dôra to Nely Sorel doesn't allow her to change her skin or erase the past of the girl she was without the love of a family.

> This was helped a lot by that crazy life, everything uncertain and different, and the company of the people, and the affection of Mr Brandini, who was paternal, perhaps a bit of a shameless father; and that quiet friendship of Estrela, without lies or illusions. (QUEIROZ, 2004, p.139).

This past that binds her to her birthplace is also expressed in other forms of memory, such as correspondence, "letters" and "telegrams", which do not allow her to lose contact with her homeland. "(...). I'm writing you these simple lines to give you our news and ask for yours, (...) but Dorinha is your own mother, aren't you coming to visit her?" (QUEIROZ, 2004, p.260.261). Even though she thinks she has broken the umbilical cord, Dôra hates everything she has experienced. This new form of the narrative shows that there is no totality in the formation of the character's conscience. Dôra is not affirmative when she denies going to the Soledade farm. She uses "didn't want to", *"(No, my God, I didn't want to go there, not even with a candle in my hand, not even if they called me, forced me...!)"* (QUEIROZ, 2004, p.264).

Memory is also marked beyond the character's speech by the letters she receives with news from home. From a formal point of view, the novel absorbs these narrative forms, the letters, the telegrams, as a new way of marking memory that goes beyond the character's direct narrative discourse, while at the same time demonstrating that Dôra's conscience still lacks autonomy. When she meets Comandante[3] she falls in love and gets married. In the last chapter of the book, "The Commander's Book", Dôra begins to live a subordinate life, searching for her family, for a home as a refuge and at the same time contemplating her childhood memories.

In **A BEATA MARIA DO EGITO,** published in 1958, Rachel de Queiroz presents us with a new form of storytelling, a scenic text that, according to Socorro Acioli, was born,

> According to the author herself, the story of her grandmother's *Flos Sanctorum,*

---

[3] The Commander, an unscrupulous man who had a "demon" name, *Asmodeu,* as he justifies: "Precisely, he's a demon" (QUEIROZ, 1975, p.231).

also called Rachel's *Flos Sanctorum, was the story* of the saint of each day. It so happened that, on one of these pages, Rachel learnt the story of a nun who sold her body to buy freedom (ACIOLI, preface to the book).

The text is divided into three acts and four scenes. In it we have a story portraying the tradition of the beatas of Juazeiro do Norte, Ceará. The plot features a beata as the main character: a "girl", "pretty", "with straight hair in braids", "dressed in a cassock tied around her waist by a cord".

The story takes place in a police station room. Here, the police are planning to invade Juazeiro because Father Cícero has not recognised the elected mayor. Beata appears, a threat to the policemen's plans. Beata moves into a masculine environment, creating a conflict in that place. Through the drama, we realise the presence of women and the power they play in the social clash. In this tangle of social voices, it is the voice of the female character, characterised by Beata, that stands out; even though she is imbued with an identity fragmented by a life ideology that runs through an idealised memory, which is transformed according to the paths she chooses. Beata lives in a dramatic universe, yet we see in her an intense will to live and, at the same time, a thirst for human communion as she fights for what she believes in.

The play is polite in its discourse, even though it is transgressive, it is characterised in a way that is coherent with the religious context and social problems, with an emphasis on religious fanaticism. Thus, we see that the subjects of enunciation interact in the construction of the dialogue which, according to Bakhtin (2006), the simplicity and transparency of what the character enunciates allows for the construction of the classic form of verbal communication. The Beata is determined and manages to recruit a band of men to go to Juazeiro, as we see in this dialogue:

> CABO (confidential) - I've heard that there are more than a dozen men from the city alone who are willing to accompany the Blessed and go to Juazeiro!
> I know very well who they are! (Angry.) But only if they come out of hiding! And don't let them play with me, because the first one I arrest is atai Beata! (QUEIROZ, 2005, p.164).

The lieutenant was in charge of the police station, and he was responsible for all the demands made by Colonel Chico Lopes, a representative of the government and a large landowner. As a representative of the people, the Beata is the character who leads the rebellion. Her actions and devotion to Father Cícero expose religious fanaticism and the exclusion and misfortune of thousands of miserable people. The play shows the conflict between law and religion, between the profane and the sacred. The central role of women, once again in Rachel de Queiroz's narratives, highlights the social insertion of women, always characterised by strength, courage and leadership.

> CABO LUCAS *(from the door, addressing the* TENANT.) - Excuse me, Lieutenant. Beata is coming. Just come.
> Let me in.
> (...).
> BEATA - Did you send for the soldiers?
> TENANT: (steps forward) - No, it was me. I'm the police chief!" (QUEIROZ, 2005, p.137).

From the construction of the saint to the prostitute, the Blessed takes on a complex configuration whose foundations lie in a patriarchal, rural, illiterate and fanatical society. This is the world she exposes. A non-coastal Brazil. The Brazil of backwardness. And once again, misery and the scrapping of the human being are in evidence.

> TENANT: *(doesn't want to listen, hugs her again.)* - Don't make a fuss! (...)! Forget that shroud - forget that it's holy... (...).
> BEATA: *(without resisting)* - John... If you promise...
> TENANT: *Don't* talk! I know I'm mad! I know it's a crime... a sin... a saint! *(holds her face between his hands, whispers)* Maria... Maria! (QUEIROZ, 2005, p.170).

Always driven by a principle of justice, the Blessed's cause is linked to Rachel's other protagonists. Characters governed by an ethic, a cause, a sense of justice, loneliness and suffering as they seek new horizons, aiming for new values in themselves:

> BEATA: - I don't care what you think. I just wish you'd let me go.
> TENANT: - But no! I saw it, I felt it... I knew you! You were a girl! No man had ever touched you. Tell me, isn't that right? You never... Never, did you?
> BEATA: - Never. You know. And now - after everything - you think I'm different? You didn't touch me. It was like the sun through the window! (QUEIROZ, 2005, p.178).

When she expresses herself in direct speech, Beata uses a metaphor to justify her behaviour and make herself understood to the lieutenant: *"it was like the sun through the glass!" In other words,* by submitting to the lieutenant's whims, she had in mind that nothing would change her ideals; at that moment, she is aware of being exploited and even though she is oppressed, she feels that everything would be worth it at that moment. Drawing inferences from Chevallier and Gheerbrant, we realise that:

> (...) the sun represents Durkheim's **social oppression,** Freud's *censorship,* from which social tendencies, civilisation, ethics and all that is important in being derive. Its range of values extends from the *super* negative, which crushes the being with prohibitions. Principles, rules or prejudices, to the *ideal of the* positive *ego,* the superior image of oneself whose greatness we seek to achieve. Therefore, the star of the day situates the being in its policed or sublimated life, it represents the face that the personality presents in its highest psychic syntheses, at the level of its

> greatest demands, its highest aspirations, its strongest individualisation, or failure made of pride or delirium of power. (CHEVALLIER. GHEERBRANT. 1998, p. 839-840).

For Beata, no matter how hard they tried to stop her from achieving her goals, they couldn't. Her conscience is clear and shows that the truth and the answers to her actions can only be found in faith and in defence of Father Cícero. The relationship between identity and memory makes the self-referential discourse explicit, being projected as a significant totality, because by giving in to the whims of the Lieutenant, the values she believes in are shattered in the face of a context of purity, breaking with social and especially religious paradigms.

Could it be that the Blessed is a "postmodern subject" who, according to Hall (2011), is decentralised from Enlightenment and social ideals and fragmented into various identities? Contradicting what she believes in: religious values? In this context, we realise that the relationship between identity and memory invokes a past, an origin that manifests itself in one's being, as a fragmented subject, which according to Hall;

> Identities seem to invoke an origin that resides in a historical past with which they continue to maintain a certain correspondence. They have to do, however, with the question of utilising the resources of history, language and culture to produce not what we are, but what we take ourselves to be (HALL, 2002, p.109).

To this end, according to Bergson (2011), our body is considered to be the centre of actions and in it images are received and transformed according to the realities of each being. Identity is therefore differentiated as a category in relation to the Humanities and Social Sciences. Because, in terms of gender and religion, it is linked to the innermost being. In the character Beata, this is visible, because she builds her identity, constitutes it as cultural values, and manifests in her trajectory what she has learnt and heard. In her speech, she demonstrates aesthetic coherence and her connection between generation and generation. History is individualised and perpetuated according to her way of living and acting. As we can see.

> BEATA: - They're pilgrims! Bandits are those who don't fear God! *(pause.)* Colonel Chico Lopes, it's written in the Tablets of the Law: whoever hurts will also be hurt. God is good, but when he wants to punish, he puts a fiery sword in the hand of his angels. You call me a saint with mockery on your lips... No, I'm not a saint, but I listen to the voice of the saints! I have a mission to fulfil. It was faith in the Mother of Sorrows, protector of Juazeiro, that armed my pilgrims (QUEIROZ, 2005, p. 193).

We see in Beata, as well as a fragmented identity, a memory full of symbolic feelings, like traits acquired over the course of a lifetime, traits that are mixed between the present and the past and that border on religious extremism. This memory is filled with collective and individual stories that for the character are full of meanings and values. Values for which she fights and which justify her very existence.

In **Memorial de Maria Moura** (1992) we have the representation of a second female voice. Marialva, a character who also tells her story. Although she is not the protagonist, she participates in and witnesses Maria Moura's experience. We can see in this character a configuration based on opposition to the image of Maria Moura, because there is a certain erasure in her actions. She's a character who lets herself be led by her brothers, Tonho and Irineu: "You could say that she's going to end up an old woman. She lives in our house. And there's the saying: he who eats from my pirão, takes from my belt. You have to do as you're told." (QUEIROZ, 2000, p.49).

Marialva is fatherless and motherless and lives under the yoke of her brothers who, because they are men, take it upon themselves to act and think according to their precepts. In this sense, the character represents the naive, sweet and fragile woman of patriarchal society. Marialva's existence is limited to her passion for Valentin, marriage and motherhood. "My face was on fire, no-one in my life had ever spoken to me like that." (QUEIROZ, 2000, p.73).

When making inferences about dreams, Bergson infers that; "Dreams and alienation don't seem to be very different (...), dreams perfectly imitate alienation." (BERGSON, 2011, p. 204). (BERGSON, 2011, p. 204) In this sense, Marialva embodies the materiality of the "affirmative" female being, according to the standards of patriarchal society. She doesn't question, nor does she take a stand to counter the impositions she suffers. Marialva represents the consolidation of women in patriarchal society. In her, submission becomes her greatest reference point.

> I was already crying because I missed him, because I felt sorry for myself, because I felt angry; because I felt bound by the will of others as if I were a rope. Ah, I still couldn't believe that one day I would be able to free myself from the Firm, from Tonho, from the house of the Black Marias. Get to know the world. Valentin could do that for me. Only him - who else? (QUEIROZ, 2000, p. 134).

From Marialva's experience, we have time on two planes of waiting: in the foreground, the wait for Valentin, between dreams and hopes, and the realisation of the wedding, the formation of the family: "I think I was a bit dizzy during the whole wedding. I don't remember anything the priest said in the sermon, there was a moment when I cried." (QUEIROZ, 2000, p.141). In the background, pregnancy, waiting for her son Xandó. This is the summary of a lifetime of getting married and becoming a mother: "I spent those days as if I were enchanted. Sleeping Beauty, Princess Magalona (....). And the worst thing was that with the fainting also came the nausea, the entojos, as Mrs Aldenora used to say." (QUEIROZ, 2000, p. 286).

Marialva's narrative in **Memorial de Maria Moura** is affirmative in relation to the prevailing codes.

Marialva lives by waiting, by accepting impositions. In the structure of the novel, this narrative contextualises the prevailing order, the limits of the female experience in the countryside, Maria Moura's space of action.

In this way, we can see that Brazilian literature, with the presence of Rachel de Queiroz, is taking a new look at women's writing, which demonstrates a restlessness when it comes to discussing gender, since the characters we are analysing here surprise the reader because, as female characters, they act and take on responsibilities that are contradictory to those of their time.

To think about Rachel's writing as a genre is to reflect on the role of the woman author who also lived in the midst of a patriarchal and conservative society. In this way, we can infer that all the boldness, in a way, that exists in the characters she created, comes from questioning, which, transported into fiction, breaks with the conventional way of life that Rachel herself lived. In this sense, the novelist's critical thinking translates into her characters breaking with tradition, as we see in the characters we are analysing here through their memorial discourse, which contributes to a transformation based on ideals of freedom. These are female characters who submit to the transgression of values, be they moral, social or ethical.

2. FREEDOM AND MEMORY IN THE MAKING

MARIA MOURA'S SPEECH

Our starting point for problematising the configuration of memory is the study of the novel **Memorial de Maria Moura** (1992) by Rachel de Queiroz, published in 1992. This novel presents us with a first-person narrative. At the level of the narrator, we realise that in narrating, Maria Moura triggers herself. In terms of the character, we have the paths she has lived. As the novel is constructed, it is the character herself who, through the image-remembrance, re-visits the past in the present and, through discourse, her trajectory is revealed as a testimony of herself.

This is the frontier on which Maria Moura's narrative is placed, presenting a perception of the "I" constructed by memory. **Memorial de Maria Moura,** with its first-person narrative focus, presents the narrator with a self strongly marked by her vision, or rather, by the construction of the image she wants of herself, either through her dreams and feelings, or through her actions. From this point of view, we see a being in transformation, as the character has a remarkable life trajectory in the deepest sense of being. In order to achieve her goals, she goes through uncertain times and suffering. As a child, which is the beginning of the memoir, she loses her father. Living with her stepfather after her mother's death, she suffers abuse. This broken childhood is the starting point of her memoir. In this sense, the memoir takes on the fullness of an entire life which, when narrated, makes the character an accomplice and confessor of herself. Maria Moura justifies herself at every turn through a discourse founded on the status of absolute truth.

The character brings with her a historical remnant of the word and, for this reason, her discourse stands out, she dialogues by speaking of others, allowing the persuasive interior of the word to convey what she wants and where she wants to go. We can see this in Bakhtin (2010);

> Each word implies a certain singular conception of the listener, their perceptual background, a certain degree of responsibility and distance. All this is very important for understanding the historical life of the word. Ignoring these aspects and nuances leads to the reification of the word, the extinction of its natural dialogism (BAKHTIN, 2010, p.146).

In this way, the character's speech favours the objectification of the word, of course, in a new dimension. Maria Moura speaks about herself and is part of a struggle, an arena on an ideological level. A discourse that mobilises the image she wants of the self, and the possible image for the other. This is the dialogical orientation of her discourse, in that the image she projects of the "I" is permeated by the discourse of others, in a mutual interaction. For Henri Bergson (2011), images are also, at the same time, memory, because it is through images that memory arises in our bodies as events and these, in turn, characterise our actions with the environment, either from the point of view of the image-remembrance or by remythologising it as an image-action.

> And I made up my story to tell the old man, in a way that he could understand. - Don't you see - I said - I'm here dressed in these men's clothes, by force, to hide from my enemies. You knew right away that I'm a girl - a family girl, right? I was expelled from my farm by some executioner cousins who wanted to take possession of what was mine when they saw me orphaned of father and mother. They did everything they could to get me off my farm and finally set fire to my house. I ran away, terrified, and called these comrades to come with me; the intention of those wretches was to burn me to death inside my house. (QUEIROZ, 2000, p. 116).

Thus, it is through the body that memories take up the past, inserting it into the present, into old and new perceptions.

> The memory of the body, made up of all the sensory-motor systems that habit has organised, is therefore an almost instantaneous memory on which the true memory of the past serves as a basis (...). On the other hand, in effect, the memory of the past presents the sensory-motor mechanisms with all the memories capable of guiding them in their task and directing the motor reaction in the direction suggested by the lessons of experience. (BERGSON, 2011, p. 178).

Memory is configured through remembrance, as if the narrator were saying "I remember" in the present tense, growing old in the Serra dos Padres, in possession of her Condado. At the level of the utterance, the fabric of memory locates the time of childhood, of loss, of abandonment. This is the beginning of everything. From the outset, his memories establish the discursive code of survival and violence, through actions that express the limit between theft, murder and banditry.

Memorial (from the Latin *memorialis*) relating to memory, in other words, it is the writing of memories, which means writing that relates memorable facts. Making inferences, Nelly Novais Coelho (2001) emphasises:

> The term memorial points to history: in its literal sense, it means a written record of the past lived (or known) by someone, who evokes it and eternalises it in time through writing. Maria Moura points to myth: it unites the emblematic name of Woman (from the biblical Virgin Mary) with the mythical ballast of the Moor (or moira): the Greek goddesses who weave the destiny of men. The three decisive moments of human life depend on them: birth, marriage and death, just as they are decisive in the novel (COELHO, 2001, p. 553).

Memorial brings a story from a lived past. **Maria Moura's Memorial** evokes the substantiated experience of a woman: Maria Moura. In the practice of the violence suffered, the conquest of the land, the refusal to marry, the unrequited love, the suffering of having to have the man she loved (Cirino) killed, in short, events that guide an entire life transform this Memorial into the shattering of a given established order and a prevailing time. The time of the lived in the face of the time of enunciation moves the articulation of discourse as a perception of self.

When it comes to memory, at the level of enunciation, the narrator reconstructs her past, establishing a discursive communication link in time, constructing her complex identity and reconstructing her own history, assuming an identity that is also discursive. According to Bakhtin: "(...). The utterance is a link in the chain of discursive communication and cannot be separated from the preceding links that determine it both from the outside and from the inside, generating in it direct responsive attitudes and dialogical resonances." (BAKHTIN, 2006, p.300). So, in this line of reasoning, we realise that the character, when enunciating through words, interacts mutually through ideological threads.

The concept of word is being used in the sense proposed by Bakhtin (2010) in the chapter **The person who speaks in the novel** (BAKHTIN, 2010, p.134-163). For the theorist, the man who speaks in the novel is essentially social, historically concrete, in other words, the image of his word. This is the word thought of as a particular point of view on the world, in its social significance. As an ideologue, this person who speaks, Maria Moura,

proposes an order founded on differences in the patriarchal base in which Marialva and the Beata survive and refer to. Maria Moura's speech dialogically opposes Marialva's (and the Beata do Egito's) understanding of the world. This is the dialogism manifested in the fragmentation of the world and ideologies, considering Marialva and Maria Moura. Every character expresses an ideological position, more or less original, and a conception of the world. In this conception of the world, the aspiration is always for social significance and acceptance. In "Pai dizia", Maria Moura seeks authority and otherness for the consciousness she expresses and transmits. As a speaker, she reworks the words of others, the dialogical condition of language and our existence. Visibly, Maria Moura manifests a historical and ideological consciousness. She doesn't assume naivety.

> The lands of the Serra dos Padres, everything fresh, a waterhole running between the rocks. Pai talked so much, I wish I'd seen it. There was the issue with the squatters; but, from what Pai said, the worst of them had already died. (...) seeing me wanting to start that war, with only four men and two horses, a donkey and three old guns.... But that was only the beginning (QUEIROZ, 2000, p. 79-83).

The thought of the world is constituted as Bakhtin says; "(...) - the speaking subject and his word determine all forms of transmission and representation of another's word (...)." (BAKHTIN, 2010, p.151). And this subject-speaker is the result of a social-historical and ideologically influenced process, which transforms him and marks his discourse. Given that, in this process, individuals are interpellated into speaking-subjects, into subjects of discourse, by the discursive formations that they represent in language, the ideological formations that correspond to them.

In Maria Moura, these images are developed through discourse at all times, mediated by the perception between past and present time, between what was left behind and how I see it now. In Bergsonian theory, remembrance is motivated and involuntary, the stimuli (which bring back the memory) are provoked by objects outside the body. These stimuli cause the movement of molecules that vary according to the object and its nature, causing changes in perception through images propagated by the brain. But Bergson makes it clear that "the body does not contribute directly to representation, neither in perception, nor in memory, nor in the higher operations of the spirit" (BERGSON, 2011, p.253). It is necessary to consider that the body in itself is not a "mathematical procedure in space, that its virtual actions are complicated and impregnated by real actions, or, in other words, that there is no perception without affection" (BERGSON, 2011, p.60). This affection is nothing more than the mixture of internal and external images, in other words, perception in the initial procedures of constitution.

Maria Moura is only present through the memorial discourse. The first person means that the narrative is assumed by a specific sender in spatial and temporal circumstances. According to Halbwachs (2006), individual memory is based on collective memory, because these memories are constituted within the thinking of a group. And even though individual memories are outside of us, all it takes is the awakening of the necessary forces for this individual memory to return to the past and be reconfigured within the collective memory. In this sense, the narrator's discourse is shaped by memories that have been internalised as a group, family, country (even as a child); and this heritage is part of and constitutes a cultural system. In contrast to Halbwachs, following Bergson's criteria (2011), we can say that memory is impossible without the present. It is the perception of the present that brings the memory of the past, and this perception occurs in the individuation of the subject: "It was now my turn." (QUEIROZ, 2000, p. 81).

Maria Moura's memory is essentially an individual memory, because when she narrates, memories and experiences are selected, establishing relationships on the level of representation. Notably, in this process of interaction, as a social being, Todorov (2003) infers that this subject, in evoking the past, becomes a word-action, an enunciated subject. "(...). I kept dreaming of that freedom. My girlish dreams weren't girlish dreams; Mother was scandalised. Because now I was free." (QUEIROZ, 2000, p.66, 87).

In Bergson (2011), we see a subject that develops from the "image - memory", in a process of communication that passes through the spirit. As a social being, we need a universe and, in this universe, perception and image, filters of the body, are selected by the brain, as we can see:

> If external perception in fact provokes movements on our part that outline it, our memory directs the old images that resemble it and whose outline has already been traced by our movements to the received perception (BERGSON, 2011, p.114,115).

There is a movement in the character's perception, a whole past of images is recalled in Maria Moura's memory, and this occurs not in a space, but precisely in an elapsed, historical and individual time:

> Lying in the bush, looking at the stars in the dark sky, I would remember Grandpa's conversations, the stories he told me so many times, so many times. He started telling them when I was a little girl (...) Then, as a young woman, I heard the same stories, now repeated by Father, when he visited his relatives. And much more explained than at the time when I still couldn't understand." (QUEIROZ, 2000, p.87)

The past is an elapsed time, the present is an elapsed time, in that both converge in an extension in which the past is configured in the present. However, it is memory that configures the "image", "sensation" and "memory" of a past-present.

> What I call my present is my attitude towards the immediate future, my imminent action. My past only becomes an image, and therefore at least a nascent sensation, which is capable of collaborating with this action, of inserting itself into this attitude, in a word, of becoming useful; but as soon as it becomes an image, the past leaves the state of pure memory and becomes confused with a certain part of my present (BERGSON, 2011, p.164).

When investigating the phenomenon of perception, as a tool of images captured by the brain, Bergson (2011) conceptualises pure perception as a total subjective element, lacking the well-known memory, limited and devoid of memories, especially those that are more intense, unusual. This pure perception is characteristic of every context of received images. Characterised by all "sensations, our perceptions are what the actual action of our body is to its possible or virtual action." (2011, p.58).

With regard to time in the phenomenon of perception, Bergson (2011) argues that it is instantaneous, at the exact moment the image is received, because the next moment it is already a memory, building a new image that will never be complete. But the more instantaneous it is, the more real it is. As we can see:

> I made an effort to discover in that new creature the angry young penitent from so
> many years ago (...). - Who are you, sir? Do you have business with me? (...). My
> God, I think I remember that face... (...). All I had going for me at that moment was
> the anger that came over me at such impudence. But even then the blood ran from
> my face, my stomach tightened. I tried to pretend I didn't remember anything (...).
> Then I forced myself to look at his face, right in the face, and I tried to pretend that,
> only after looking closely, I remembered that morning in the church. (QUEIROZ,
> 2000, p. 10-12).

We repeat in this quote that Maria Moura meets her confessor again and at first denies knowing him, but the images of the moment she experienced at the time cause the memory to become established. In the general context, these perceptions and images go through a selection process in the brain, like "something inexplicable", as Bergson explains: "What you have to explain, therefore, is not how perception is born, but how it is limited, since it would be, by right, the image of the whole, and it is reduced, in fact, to what interests you" (2011, p.28). In this sense, we see how the character observes what is happening around her, in the presence of her confessor, questions and experiences that moment of the present in the past or the past re-signified in the present.

> It was hard and it was slow. But now I was standing on the porch of my sturdy
> house, looking out at the world around me: down at the várzea, up at the mountains
> and, on both sides, the perambeira trees at the foot of the hill. (...) With all this, my
> greatest pride was the house. (...) And then the house itself, spreading out from the
> sides; in front, the wide porch, with its well-cut aroeira posts, the tiled floor.
> (QUEIROZ, 2000, p. 294).

In this analysis, it is difficult to establish the exact limits of memories and perceptions, so Bergson himself comments that:

> Perception is never a simple contact between the spirit and the present object; it is
> impregnated with memory-images that contemplate it, interpreting it. The memory-
> image, in turn, participates in the "pure memory" that it begins to materialise, and
> in the perception in which it tends to incarnate: considered from this last point of
> view, it could be defined as nascent perception (BERGSON, 2011, p. 109).

Perception is situated in time and space, with no difference between the present and the past, because what is perceived is its constant extension into the present. Memory can be defined as instantaneous perception, which for Bergson is twofold:

> (....) once fixed in the organism, it is nothing more than the set of intelligently
> assembled mechanisms that ensure a suitable response to the various possible

> interpellations. It makes us adapt to the present situation, and the actions we take
> [...] more habit than memory, it plays on our past experience, but doesn't evoke its
> image. The other is true memory. Coextensive with consciousness, it retains and
> aligns all our states one after the other as they occur, giving each fact its place, (...)
> date (...) (2011, p. 124).

The author tries to analyse the presuppositions of memory up to the extremes of dualism in order to re-establish the relationship between spirit and matter, making it clear that memory-memory is a fraction of remembrance which, in turn, makes up the domain of the spiritual and extends through the cerebral procedure, where it materialises.

> (...) images over time as they are produced, and as if our body, with what surrounds
> it, were no more than one of these images, the last one that we obtain at every
> moment by making an instantaneous cut in becoming in general. In this cut, our
> body occupies the centre (BERGSON, 2011, p. 83).

In this process of putting images together, objects are recognised. Memories, on the other hand, cease to be mere representations as a perception of the spirit that imposes certain durations on them. Bergson (2011) also argues that there are "two memories, one of which imagines and the other repeats, the second of which can replace the first and often even give the illusion of it" (BERGSON, 2011, p. 89). So, in memories, consequently, the images are spontaneous and sudden, yet "it hides itself at the slightest movement of voluntary memory". And although "it remains capricious in its manifestations and, since the memories it brings have something of a dream about them, it is rare that its more regular intrusion into the life of the spirit does not profoundly disturb the intellectual equilibrium" (BERGSON, 2011, p. 97). Memories and images are formed by "memory par excellence", which can be stored by the spirit. Memory is something alien to matter, but it highlights the reality of the spirit through the phenomenon of remembrance. This, in turn, presents needs, as the author describes:

> (...) memories, in order to be actualised, need a motor coadjuvant, and they require,
> in order to be recalled, a kind of mental attitude that is itself part of a bodily attitude.
> Thus verbs, whose essence is to express imitable actions, are precisely the words
> that a bodily effort will allow us to reach when the function of language is about to
> be lost: on the other hand, proper names, being of all words the most distant from
> those impersonal actions that our body is capable of sketching, are those that a
> weakening of the function would reach first (BERGSON, 2011, p. 139).

In this context, the idea of pure memories is concentrated in the depths of the memory, so they are presented together with the images capable of implanting themselves in the motor system. "As these memories acquire the form of a more complete, more concrete and more conscious representation, they tend to become confused with the perception that attracts them or whose framework they adopt" (BERGSON, 2011, p.146). These memories are present in Maria Moura's memory, since the character revisits and ratifies her perception, as we can see. "- I won't deny to you that I have a plan in my head. In my head and in my heart, I might add. It's a very old idea that I've carried with me since the days of my late grandfather." (QUEIROZ, 2000, p. 82).

In this sense, Rossi (2010) says that remembering means a "voluntary search among the contents of the soul". And in order to make this search, one must have deliberative capacity, because in remembering, the subject "fixes by inference what they have previously seen", "heard" or "experienced". As he himself defines it: "(...). Memory is for men and animals, reminiscence is only human." (ROSSI, 2010, p.16).

The narrative presents a plot that takes place in the middle of the 19th century, in rural, northeastern Brazil. It features Maria Moura who ventures into the miserable backlands. The journey from Limoeiro to the long-dreamed-of Serras dos Padres, lands that Maria Moura had inherited from her grandfather and father, creates a transgressive and strong image. The starting point and the conquest is Casa Forte, her county. The character, with all the complexity inherent in a being who breaks with antagonistic forces, seeks her social place through the possession of land: property. As a past, memory is contained in the present, inaugurating an ancestry of the character and the land: land that was her grandfather's, her father's desire, Maria Moura's possession. For Todorov, "if the entire present was already contained in the past, the past, in turn, is present in the present (...). But the present must become the past so that another present can help us understand it." (TODOROV, 2003, p.183-184). The narrator's present visits the character's past-present as a form of learning and identity.

> I don't know what was in my voice or on my face, but they agreed without stopping to think. Then I got up from the floor, asked for João Rufo's knife, sharpened like a razor - I pulled it out: my hair, which was down my back in a thick braid; I put the blunt side of the knife against the back of my neck and, strand by strand, I cut the hair at neck level. I knotted the braid and handed it to João Rufo, along with the knife. - Keep this hair in your saddlebag." (QUEIROZ, 2000, p.84)

Maria Moura, as a character, is aware of her choice, of this link with her grandfather's and father's past, with the reintegration and rescue of Serra dos Padres: "One day I'm going to take revenge on those bat-like souls of the Marias Pretas. But that will take time (...). Just like that, one day they'll pay me back. One day." (QUEIROZ, 2000, p. 125).

Her choice implies leaving her home of origin, her "corner of the world" as Bachelard (2000) puts it, a place where she learnt "oneiric values" and lived the dreams that will lead her to a new home, that of desires. The character Maria Moura is part of a world seen (and shown) by the narrator as hostile and limiting to the role of women. Belonging to the patriarchal world, the narrator brings into the performative scheme of enunciation, the problem of action, and the problem of the word, of the character's dignity: "You can leave with your soldiers, your role (...). I can only leave my house by force and tied up." (QUEIROZ, 2002, p.38). In the performative scheme, the enunciation is already the fulfilment of the action, which is always self-referential, takes itself and reflects the consciousness of the act of narrating. The story of the "I" shows the transformation of the girl into the Moura woman.

> I had planned everything, the defence and the fire (...). When it was my time, I just tried to take a deep breath and smell that freedom. It didn't hurt so much when I waited for the fire in the Limoeiro house; after all, the time had come for my great dream to be fulfilled. The lands of the Serra dos Padres, everything fresh, water flowing between the rocks. Father talked so much, it was the same thing I had already seen (...) (QUEIROZ, 2002, p.7).

2.1-From the inner plane to the plane of action: metamorphosis and estrangement

In the eyes of the reader, Maria Moura's conflict is understandable, given that inside her there is a time lived, a memory, an assumed responsibility. The narrator also has a finished vision of Maria Moura. Drawing inferences from Walnice Vilalva (2012), she asserts that "However bad the outcome of Maria Moura's actions, the reasons that led her "to act in one way and not another" (VILALVA, 2012, p.221), point to the image of a narrator who, when talking about herself, speaks from an apologetic perspective. Speaking in the first person is always performative, according to which the intention makes the word the sublime effect of the "I".

> I stayed up all night thinking about it; in the end I decided to find a way to get Irineu into my hands and then teach him. As it was, until I finished him off. Or capar, as Father used to say, talking about his enemies: 'He can only be capped'.
> I had to bait him. But I couldn't cheat on the bait, because they were as bad as they were clever. It had to be very good bait that they could swallow well (QUEIROZ, 2000, p.196).

From this perspective, Maria Moura presents us with her inner world, everything she learnt from her grandfather, and then from her father, in a temporal unfolding that takes place in ("Faço como meu Pai faria"). The past becomes the character's present-action, returning to the present, engaging the continuity of time. "(...). And regaining that possession was my grandfather's dream on his father's side, and after his father's, and after his grandfather's death, it became my father's dream." (QUEIROZ, 2000, p.21).

> -I'll warn you: it might be worse with me than with a corporal and a sergeant. You
> have to obey me with your eyes closed. You have to forget that I'm a woman - that's
> why I'm wearing these men's trousers. (...). Then I got up from the floor, asked for
> João Rufo's knife, sharpened like a razor - I pulled my hair down my back in a thick
> braid; I put the blind side of it against the back of my neck and, strand by strand, I
> cut my hair at neck level. (...). - Now Sinhazinha do Limoeiro is gone. Who's here
> is Maria Moura, your boss, heiress to a date in Fidalga Brites' sesmaria, in Serra dos
> Padres, let's go and harness up the animals (QUEIROZ, 2000, p. 84).

Sinhazinha, from Limoeiro, gives birth to a new young woman dressed as a man, Maria Moura. Her transformation into Maria Moura makes the gang feel strange because of the way she dresses and speaks like a man.

> I put on a pair of trousers that had belonged to Dad, so I could ride more freely. It
> fitted me perfectly, I knew. (...) I wore my father's jacket on top to hide my bigger
> waist (QUEIROZ, 2000, p.84).

In this break with her orphaned past, the narrator informs us of the formation of the leader, the maturing of Maria Moura in the space of the war, of the journey, of the struggle to Serra dos Padres. As heiress to the land, heiress to power, her journey locates a point of departure and a point of arrival.

> - There are no women here, only your boss. If I tell you to shoot, you shoot; if I
> tell you to die, you die. Those who disobey pay dearly. So dearly and so quickly
> that they won't even have time to repent.
> - Now the little lady from Limoeiro is over. Who's here is Maria Moura, your boss,
> heiress to a date in the sesmaria of Fidalga Brites, in Serra dos Padres. Let's go and
> harness up the animals (QUEIROZ, 2000, p.84).

The character's individuality sets the tone for problematising social roles (man/woman), the patriarchal structure in areas of isolation and precariousness. Between banditry, violence and backwardness, the sertão is covered with a critical awareness on the part of the narrator. To live in this sertão, you need to have strength and fame: "I had a lot to fight for in this world outside - because I was convinced that in this life, if you don't fight for what you want, you end up. I wanted to be strong. I wanted fame. I wanted revenge." (QUEIROZ, 2000, p.121).

The individualism manifested in free direct speech, as the character's conscience, shows Maria Moura's self-centred, selfish character. According to Nelly Novais Coelho (2001, p.554), she prefigures the "ambiguity and creative/transforming force of the Feminine." It is in the pursuit of her objective, her goal, her dreams, that we get closer to an affirmative "I". In the syntagma "I had to have", constant in Maria Moura, desire anticipates possession, realisation. The discourse doubles as wanting and having at the same time: "I had to have gold to have power. The land, the luxury, the power to command people (...)" (QUEIROZ, 2000, p.177).

From this perspective, the character's words are based on the representation of desire, establishing a relationship between subjectivity and the exteriority of action. According to Bakhtin (2010), both actions and words are underlined by ideology, so the character acts and lives their own "conception of the world".

According to Halbwaches (2006), individual memory is not entirely "isolated" or "closed"; in order to "evoke" the past, the subject needs to revisit the "memories of others" and thus transport themselves to points outside themselves. On the journey to the Serra dos Padres, amid various assaults and violence, Maria Moura retraces the path she had heard about from her grandfather since she was a child. The memory drives her desire for the land.

"- There it is! There it is! (...). - And I pointed with trembling hands. There's the Serra dos Padres!" (QUEIROZ, 2000, p.230). The conquest of the land compensates for the suffering, feeds the ego and strengthens the character. The construction of the long-dreamed-of "Casa Forte", the house of desire, symbolises the greatness of the time that has passed between her birthplace and the house of desire and, in it, the maturity that Maria Moura has reached.

In the adventures and adventures, the narrator's configuration indicates the heroism and truth expressed in Maria Moura's actions. The elevated affirmation of the character Moura is a constant that leads to the fulfilment of being. From Sinhazinha to Maria Moura and, finally, Dona Moura. In the names, the process of renaming the character absorbs the gradual process of recognition and learning undergone by the character. From girl to Dona, owner of the lands of Serra dos Padres. The time marked by the character's actions indicates desire, conquest and ageing. Her narrator learns the importance of patience, "(...). - I didn't lack patience; neither patience nor hope." (QUEIROZ, 2000, p. 271). And so they arrive at Serra dos Padres, and hope, manifested in her speech, takes up residence in her heart, in the memory of a mature woman. Moura observes the finished "Casa Forte" from the porch. This is her creation. According to Bergson (2011) it is in consciousness that perception is constituted and that the answers to what we are looking for are obtained according to our actions in the world.

In this observation of creation, Mrs Moura is reflected in the image she sees of the house of desire.

The dream of the land and the construction of his new world are reminiscent of what he had heard from his father when he was a child. The past becomes present. In Maria Moura, the "images - memories" are perfectly rooted in dreams, action (individual memory) and discourse as a perception and expression of subjectivity and complete individuality through non-submission.

2.2 - The lyrical being in Maria Moura

As we have already seen, the narrative in Memorial de Maria Moura sets out, through discourse, what is notorious in Rachel de Queiroz's works: the characterisation of female characters who are averse to marriage and social impositions. Those who appear adhering to these values are simply there to counter and further affirm the ideals of liberating the role of women in society.

As we can see, the character Maria Moura carries with her a whole memorialistic ideology that has made her great and powerful. She took on her role without accepting being defeated by anyone, even by the most sublime feeling - love. Moura could love, but without letting herself be taken over by this feeling that has the power to transform one's being.

In Maria Moura, the lyricism is reinforced in the non-acceptance of falling in love with Cirino and especially in the suffering he has caused her with his betrayal. The self-possessed character wonders how she can accept and live with someone who wants to excel in his domination. Moura doesn't consent to this. Her self is unhappy, suffering, decisions need to be made, but how? Kill Cirino? These are moments of deep anguish, but it has to be done, Cirino has to die. The decision has already been made, as we see:

> Suddenly, I couldn't hear anything else, say anything else. I ran into the bedroom and threw myself on the bed. I had tried so hard not to let him know that he was going to be killed by my hand. To do this, I invented using Valentim; I sent the knife through his back and he fell, with no time to know anything (...). The only consolation I had left was gone: him being killed without knowing he was going to die, let alone knowing that he was going to die by my command. (...) The thoughts gnawed at me inside, strangled me. I couldn't even cry. Imagine the surprise, the hatred in that heart. Hate against me! Even if it was just a flash of lightning as the knife whistled through the air, coming to pierce the chest until it reached his heart (QUEIROZ, 2000, p.460).

We see that the character's anguish, suffering and everything she goes through are strongly marked by the verbs "gnawed", "could", "buzzed" as marks of a past time that left deep feelings in her being, but at the same time we realise how ephemeral Moura's life is, because for her. "When it came to doing justice, I relied on my strength: what had to be done was done. And with such care and luck that everything worked out." (QUEIROZ, 2000, p.466). Drawing inferences from Mônica Raisa Schpun in her article *Lé, com, lé, cré com cré?* (SCHPUN, 2002, p. 180), this confrontation between Moura and Cirino is "full of rawness" and everything happens to express what exists in the power relationship between man and woman, which in Maria Moura's case, being submissive is not in her plans, and that is the great fissure in this relationship.

The dynamics that Maria Moura uses to recount her memory show the reader how perceptive she is in the unfolding of events. The character demonstrates that she doesn't care about the consequences that life may offer her, that rebellion is present in her ego, impregnated in her being. After so many struggles and sufferings, Moura could very well stay in his "county", but he doesn't. He prefers to leave in search of new things. He prefers to leave in search of new horizons, consistent with the underlying ideal of life set out by Lilith[4] , who could also have had a peaceful life living in Paradise, respecting the ideals of society at the time.

In this sense, both Moura and Lilith clearly demonstrate the ideals of liberation in the role of women in search of their rights, in showing that women also have their value and know how to lead their lives. Lilith made her choice by not accepting to be submissive to Adam, to be under him at the moment of intimacy, she preferred to leave for the red lands "hell" where she would have freedom, she would live according to her thoughts. Moura chose not to give in to the love that Cirino had to offer her, a love full of betrayals, not only with women, but especially moral betrayals;

> Locked in my room, alone, thinking about the harm that Cirino had done to me. Not that I was wrong about him, I know I wasn't. My evil was that great weakness I felt for him. I liked to call it love. But only because I thought it was beautiful and because, in love, everything is forgiven. But it wasn't love, it was worse (...). And now I - I had to face that betrayal. Not of love, which can be forgiven, but of faith. Betrayal of Maria Moura, the woman Cirino boasted about in the girls' house, who ate out of the palm of his hand (...). Who else was going to take Maria Moura at her word? To this day, Moura had never made a false statement to anyone. An enemy is an enemy, but a partner and a friend is a very different definition (QUEIROZ, 2002, p.418).

The character prefers to have him killed and continue on her adventurous way. One day, Maria Moura receives a visit from a cattle buyer. He tells her about some travellers who buy cattle to take their charque to the south. These cattle buyers travelled in gangs and with them a lot of money and weapons. In her heart, Maria Moura finds a way to start all over again, as she says: "Seu Francelino's conversation had, in a way, woken up the old Maria Moura. Or rather, a new Maria Moura, different from all the Mouras of the past, capable of embarking on a crazy adventure, perhaps with no return, perhaps with no end." (QUEIROZ, 2000, p.472).

So she prepares all the weapons, even though she is questioned by her subordinates, Moura doesn't give up on the adventure and the risks she would run, "Well, I avoided thinking about the risks of that adventure. "At the point she had reached, the risks didn't frighten her. God will see for himself." (QUEIROZ, 2000, p. 476) For her, even if she didn't receive divine protection, nothing mattered, the decision had already been made.

See (CHEVALLIER, Jean. GHEERBRANT, Alain.1998, p. 548)

Moura is aware of her capacity and her power, which she has painstakingly achieved.

So we see a character who, in his rebellion, non-acceptance and non-conformity, throws himself into an unprecedented life. For Moura, from then on, everything would be worthwhile, but what about the love of life? Drawing inferences from Bergson (2011), we can say that we need to be stripped of materialist and spiritualist concepts so that when we encounter images, they are without value. All of this is related to the body, which is both matter and image, both interior and exterior, because it is in the body that reactions take place; the body, according to Bergson, is a mediator and translator of these images:

> All these images act and govern each other in all their elementary parts according to constant laws, which I call the laws of nature, and since a perfect knowledge of these laws would certainly allow us to calculate and predict what will happen in each of these images, the future of the images must be contained in their present and nothing new must be added to them. However, there is one that prevails over the others to the extent that I know it not only from the outside, through perceptions, but also from the inside, through affections: it is my body (BERGSON, 2011, p. 11).

With this realisation formed, Moura takes a new direction in life. Together with his subordinates, they set off on an adventure. The intriguing thing is that the character leaves clues to the reader's imagination. What would be the end of her adventure, would she return to Casa Forte or not? As we can see: "(...). I took a boy with me (...); when I got to where I wanted to go, I would return the horse and the boy (...)" (QUEIROZ, 2000, p. 476). In this sense, we can see that Moura's ideals of liberation emerge in their entirety; the lyrical self is clamouring for what is beyond what the life he has lived could offer him.

In Maria Moura we see lyricism marked by a memory between coming and going. She is a character who constantly needs to reconstruct her being in order to realise her liberating intentions, because she is in the midst of a patriarchal society that subjugates the role of women. Thus, the rupture in Moura materialises in relation to this society, her self does not consent to this inequality and submission. It was no coincidence that when she left Limoeiro and took on the role of someone who would have to fight for her goals in favour of her dreams, she dressed as a man, inheriting her father's trousers and belt, cutting her hair, rebelling. With regard to cutting her hair, Walnice Nogueira Galvão[5] explains the significance of this metamorphosis very well. On the contrary, it is in this coming and going that she acquires the strength to continue her struggle in the midst of so much suffering. All this language expressed in Maria Moura demonstrates what Bakhtin (2010) says: the

---

[5] See in GALVÃO, Walnice Nogueira. The Warrior Maiden, 1998, p.169-207

person who speaks in the novel "(...) always represents a particular point of view on the world, which aspires to social significance" (BAKHTIN, 2010, p.135). It is because he aspires to this idea of liberation that Moura starts all over again, as we see:

> And if I can't stand it; if the blood that's been trodden in here kills me with poison - well, I'll die! I will die one day, after all. Everyone dies. But I want to die in my greatness (...). I jumped on the saddle. But before setting off, I bent over the horse's neck and said, looking into Duarte's eyes: - If I have to die there, I'll die and that's that. But staying here I'll die a lot more (QUEIROZ, 2002, p.421- 482).

We can see, then, that both Moura and Lilith knew how to value the ideals of freedom and power. For them, not even the risk of death makes them give up the fight, in the relations of power in a patriarchal society, and that in the midst of so much adversity, they seek freedom in their own way.

2.3 - The ideological discourse: the conquest of respect and recognition in Maria Moura

The value and perspective offered by Maria Moura's speech is intense. The character Maria Moura builds her discourse in a state of tension, opposing her tormentors and manipulating the other characters, who are very close to her socio-economic, historical, cultural and ideological background. In light of this, Bakhtin says:

> The man who speaks and his word are presented here as the fundamental object of the idea and of discourse. All the essential categories of judgement and ethical and legal assessment are correlated to the speaking subject as such: conscience ("the voice of conscience", "the inner word"), truth and lies, responsibility, the faculty to act, free confession and so on (...) (BAKHTIN, 2010, p. 149).

The word is an ideological sign, so ideology is a reflection of social structures.

In other words, if the use of discourse is ideological, there is no language without social interaction. In Maria Moura, these ideological clues become more complex, as her discourse is permeated by individual memory, which takes full responsibility for events in both her speech and actions.

Therefore, Moura, who has acquired the nature of a boss, has made her discourse a necessary, productive and effective framework for constructing her world, her reality. Moura is subordinate to her discourse and, why not, to language and history. As a character, she reveals her struggle to realise her desires and intentions. "Especially me, it was important that they respected me, that people had faith in my reputation as a woman of my word. Now I had my house ready, my cattle in the fields (...). My gold was already worth a lot (...)" (QUEIROZ, 2000, p.295).

We realise that through words, through speech, Maria Moura changes and transforms various states of affairs. By overcoming, she breaks down prejudice in a macho society in which the female sex, fragile, seems incapable. In this break with the past, the narrator haughtily configures the condition she seeks for herself, that of leader, beyond her time, living in an antagonistic space, being thrown into a prejudiced context where she would have to fight with the weapons she possesses in order to be recognised as a true leader, owner of the power that the land would give her. So we understand Mrs Moura in her individualism mediated by courage and strength.

As the story continues, Maria Moura and her gang meet a white man, a boy and a black man. The white man says he's an official of the "Imperial Government", but she doesn't even respect him, at first she just wants a leather "canastrinha", and the man gets nervous. Dona Moura is not intimidated, she shows him how strong she is to face even the "Imperial Government", and orders one of her goats to put the gun to the old man's belly: "- Zé, put the gun to the belly of the Imperial Government (...)." (QUEIROZ, 2000, p.262). Thinking of Maria Moura in a society in which women have no power and cannot manage their own, it is clear that author Rachel de Queiroz's autonomy in reporting facts, even if they are in literature or fiction, marks a concrete break with that society, because in the character Maria Moura, the "Imperial" government does not have dominion, she can and does take responsibility for commanding what is rightfully hers. As Bakhtin argues:

> The goal of assimilating the words of others takes on an even deeper and more important meaning in the process of man's ideological formation, in the exact sense of the term. Here, the word of others is no longer presented as information, indications, rules, models, etc. - it seeks to define the very foundations of our ideological attitude towards the world and our behaviour, it appears here as an *authoritative* word and as an *inwardly persuasive word* (BAKHTIN, 2010, p.142).

We understand that the character Maria Moura establishes her role of strength and domination through uninterrupted social dialogue. The discourse used by Maria Moura demonstrates an arena of social class struggle, showing the subject (Maria Moura) as a remarkable being in her environment, permeated and constituted by the discourses that surround her. Imagining the character Maria Moura on one side, and the macho society on the other, it's difficult to reach a consensus, because the conflict is evident. If the word is an arena of social struggles, the subject Maria Moura is an arena of conflicts and convergences of various discourses that surround and constitute her, and each of these discourses, when confronted, exerts a hegemonic fury. Thus, the words uttered by the character produce the effects she desires. Her discourse allows her to restore the past, think about the future and re-signify the present as an action.

> Anyway, I thought the time had come to make my big journey - that is, the pilgrimage in search of the Serra dos Padres. (...) As you can see, I had that whole route in my head. I learnt it like someone who learns a prayer, taught by Grandpa. The old man, disgusted at not having a male grandson, made me learn all about our rights on the land of Serra dos Padres, so that one day I could make my husband, or a son, recover that land that was worth more than gold, with its perennial water and fresh land. (QUEIROZ, 2000, p. 225-226).

This discourse leaves traces of structural and social inequality in a society that has historically established differences between men and women. "(...) and what we really want is to be protected, to have a boss (...). Do you think any stupid soldier is going to arrest someone who he knows is Maria Moura's bitch?" (QUEIROZ, 2000, p. 327). As a landowner, Maria Moura now enjoys respect and recognition in the socio-economic structure of the sertão, which previously belonged only to the colonels.

In this context, Joanna Courteau, in her article *The feminisation of national discourse in the work of Rachel de Queiroz* (2001), draws inferences by saying that Maria Moura,

> Playing the role of border colonel, she provides refuge and protection to those persecuted by the justice system and to the unsuccessful. With such refugees, with grandchildren of slaves, with mixed descendants of Indians, with remnants of the population of Portuguese descent and the beginnings of European immigration, she transforms her fort into a microcosm of Brazil, a paradise, a kind of multicultural quilombo, where justice and charity reign (...) (COURTEAU, 2001, p.754).

When we try to understand this whole process, supported by Bakhtinian concepts, we realise the idea that the subject is constituted by listening to and assimilating the words and discourses of others, in the various spheres of social structures. And that, therefore, the subject is seen as being imbricated in their social environment, being permeated and constituted by the discourses that surround them. It became clear that through the word, through conflicting and competing discourses, the character Maria Moura is part of an uninterrupted social dialogue because language is a social product and the subject is an active part of the social environment.

3. MEMORIAL OF MARIA MOURA AND THE AESTHETICS OF CONFESSION

The aesthetics of confession are shaped by Maria Moura's discourse which, right from the start, both because of the title of the novel - **Memorial de Maria Moura** - and because of its narrative, is supposed to be her autobiography. In the first chapter of the novel, the narrator character recounts events she has experienced that denote memory and confession, not confession because she is in dialogue with a priest, but because she is dealing with events that she has been affected by and, faced with what she will suffer as a form of revenge, she takes on the death of the evildoer without any guilt, but with courage and firmness: "Father, I confess because I have sinned? I have committed a great sin... The sin of the flesh... With a man... My stepfather! And the worst thing is that now I have to have him killed..." (QUEIROZ, 2000, p.7). Memory is recognised by the adult character's recollection of events that happened in her youth. Confession is characterised by the act of reporting a situation that society would have kept hidden. In this sense, we realise that the assumption of truth is implied as a transformative action in the form that the character would use to change the environment in which she is inserted. In Maria Moura's speech, we see the transforming presence as a passage from what would be human nature itself to a new society, through the instinct for justice.

We realise that the narrator, in talking about herself, calls for the status of truth, the inclination of the solitary voice that brings about self-knowledge, the perception of oneself in the facts, in the lived experience. In this process, memory, re-signified in the present by the narrator, brings awareness through the choice of sincerity. Confession is a discourse that doubly brings recognition of an experience that caused damage, and a feeling of guilt.

Confessing, from the Latin *confessare,* establishes the ritualistic condition of Maria Moura's speech. Confessing a lifetime means, in Maria Moura's speech, recognising herself, getting involved and finding the truth about herself in the meaning of the word, spoken, ritualised.

In addition, the trajectory of the narrative brings Maria Moura's experience into the mix of actions and times, which stands out from the other characters and in which desires, disappointments and disillusions are interwoven. From leaving her childhood home to the house of desires (O Condado), the discourse of self-enunciation strips the character of the condition of confessing through irrational discourse.

In this sense, **Memorial de Maria Moura** is largely linked to the status of sincerity defended by Rousseau in **Confessions**[6] ; insofar as the immanence of truth is permeated by the memory of a narrator who, in speaking of himself, speaks apologetically. Both **Confessions** and **Memorial de Maria Moura** feature characters who present the supremacy of the self in itself.

---

[6] ROUSSEAU, Jean-Jacques. **Confessions.** São Paulo: Edipro, 2008.

We then see the greatness of the soul of a dreamy narrator who, in narrating his adventures, commits himself to what he believes to be true, justifying himself against everyone and everything, expressing life, the contradictions of being. Thus, according to SENA (1988), Rousseau's work, with ideas that were not very clear and contradictory by the standards of the time, caused and still cause reflections in our lives, from the point of view of the "conception of life, of society, of education".

The similarity of a confessional aesthetic project between the speeches of the narrators of **Confessions** and **Memorial de Maria Moura** is due to the effect of the purity of the soul, the immanence of the heart, searching for its own being in frankness.

> On top of my apragatas, under my hat... I kept dreaming of that freedom, my girlish dreams weren't girlish dreams; Mum was scandalised (...). The fact is that I'd never done what Mum wanted in my life (...). -It wasn't that I didn't love Mum, maybe I just felt sorry for her. (...). I never quarrelled with her, only when she came to demand that I behave like a family girl, sometimes I'd reply that she didn't have the morals to impose rules on me (QUEIROZ, 2000, p.87-121).

In this way, the two narrative projects postulate an invasion of intimacy. On the one hand, "the yearning to justify a life by the same life", as Sena (1988) infers, since these narrators make it clear that their confession permeates the defence of a wronged being and their discourse is characterised by the pretension not to hide anything from anyone; on the other, life's adventures, ambition and dreams are expressions of the will. "I felt (and still feel) that I wasn't born for small things. There I really felt that I had found my corner of the world, my county." (QUEIROZ, 2000, p. 239).

Maria Moura expresses her desire for transformation as a character who seeks freedom and property at any price. As Tacca (1983, p.81) argues, the narrator begins to interact with the other. In this interaction, through the narrator's discourse, the "I" places itself before itself. And the narrative becomes a mirror and a reflected, retained, contained image of this "I". In a discourse that wants to apprehend the essence of the soul, the narrator has no interest in hiding his problems; on the contrary, he reveals his truth to the world, proudly telling his story. Moura is truthful in her own being, even in her new lifestyle, she is concerned with the essence, which shows the existential memory, the appearance has changed, but the core of the feminine being remains. "It was true. But what I didn't want was for them to see my face. The face of a woman. Even with my hair cut, I shouldn't look like a man." (QUEIROZ, 2000, p. 112).

In this existential movement of the narrator character there is a feeling marked by deep selfishness, the play of self-interest with mature ideas, she knows what she wants and how to manipulate those around her.

Moura, with this intention of conquest, reads how to develop her discourse on the other, and thus achieve her goals.

> I listened to the slave's story and made a plan. Instead of taking over the old blacks' dwelling, I could very well make them a kind of resident, or even caretaker, for us. (...) And I made up my story to tell the old man, in a way that he could understand. (QUEIROZ, 2000, p. 116)

The image we see in Maria Moura is that of a contrast between the existential female being and the being brutally transformed by an authoritarian society. The character is not transformed by desire, but by survival. The girl she was in the past no longer exists, the environment has changed her into a perverse and evil being, as we see marked in her speech by the verbs "wanted", "felt", "had" in the imperfect tense of the indicative, emphasising the memory in action of the being in the present. "I wanted to be strong. I wanted to be famous. I felt that, inside the woman I was today, there was no more room for the girl without evil." (QUEIROZ, 2000, p. 121).

If we think about the facts narrated by Maria Moura, which have nothing to do with universal truths and can only be linked to her own life, experienced in her individuality, this narrator exposes herself as she sees the world and says to the other "I" am "I" am and I don't need anyone to present themselves for me or take on my role. We realise that this narrator doesn't limit herself to the other, she thinks and acts according to her ideology from a perspective in which the coherence between world and subject predominates, "which consists of a mixture of a just awareness of one's own singularity" (WEISCHEDEL, 1999, p. 181); and every moment lived provides this character with precious information that is consigned to memory. The truth in the act of narrating and the search for the subjectivity of one's own being. TACCA (1983) says that "a character's account requires a precise angle of vision, a constant perspective, limited information." (TACCA, 1983, p. 80). We can see this in Maria Moura's narrative: she only tells what she wants to and what suits her to achieve her goals. What is evident in her discourse is that she and only she is capable of talking about herself, what is said justifies what she believes to be the pre-eminence of her own being: she knows herself, it is not up to others to know her.

This constant perspective of sincerity is born out of Maria Moura's honesty of purpose, in other words, mediated by the point of view of the person who gives it meaning. If, on the one hand, *confessing* confers intimacy to the discourse, on the other hand, it ritualises the act, the word, the experience. For Sena (1988), aesthetic sincerity is a justification. "(...). Because the key to aesthetic sincerity lies in accepting that life imitates art, but also in knowing, unlike the aestheticians, that this imitation is done in terms of lived or imagined human experiences (...)" (SENA, 1988, p.13).

The narrator, Maria Moura, is a subject of action and sensitively exposes error and suffering. Senna (1988) adds. "Crying with oneself or with the image of that self is a healthy and positive confusion." (SENA, 1988, p.13). Thus, Maria Moura expresses herself by seeking transparency as a way of freeing herself from oppressive forces, be they social or religious.

> I always felt very alone. Now, that forced intimacy with my men, them chatting, arguing, I understood that they didn't say much out of respect for me. I may have been the boss, but I was also the little lady (...) (QUEIROZ, 2000, p.87)

The configuration of this character raises questions about life, resignation to the impositions of a society that massifies the self. What is not allowed is constantly violated and becomes "self-liberation", the only path to the fullness of life. In this sense, Maria Moura finds, through reason, a constant conflict with feeling and emotion. This makes the individuality of this character conflicting and suffering. As the narrator of her own self, she configures a being who seeks to live the essence of herself, without appearances. She denies a life that shows lies and pretence in the eyes of society. From this perspective, we draw inferences from WEISCHEDEL (1999) when he talks about the "I" in Rousseau, in his article "Rousseau or The Unfortunate Sentimental Thinker", when quoting Kant alluding to Rousseau's thinking, he writes: "Rousseau discovered, in the first place, under the multiplicity of fictitious human appearances, the deeply hidden nature of man." (WEISCHEDEL, 1999). (WEISCHEDEL, 1999, p. 186). For Ligia Chiappini (2002), in her article "Rachel de Queiroz: invention of the Northeast and much more", "Rachel's utopia would be a society in which man could meet his essence - human nature - and build a society without masks." (CHIAPPINI, 2002, p. 165). In this context, **Memorial de Maria Moura,** as a narrative of the "I", embodies a project by Rachel de Queiroz. Both character and author belong to a patriarchal society with absolute power. They take responsibility for their choice, for denouncing it, and make life a constant struggle. In this context, we realise that the novelist, through the voice of the narrator character, presents in the narrative the breaking of a silence and the submission of women in human relationships, since the narrative takes place in modern times, but the facts that occurred are part of past times. Maria Moura's discourse re-dimensions life in the daily making of the narrative. Although Benjamin (2012) in **The Narrator** speaks of a certain erasure of the art of narrating, which is linked to orality. We note, however, that Rachel de Queiroz, like Machado de Assis, brings to Brazilian literature characters who narrate in the first person, denouncing and taking on the ills of society, because they immerse themselves in their own "I", both on the level of enunciation, which, as a rule, goes back to the past, as in the narrative of the character Maria Moura who, in the subtlety of her speech, we have the memory of an entire path travelled in her life, or in the enunciation in which the memorialistic portrait comes out of herself, the narrator character knows little about the other, but a lot about herself.

In this way, we can see that the narrator's memorial discourse is full of cultural tradition and, at the same time, characterised by human degradation and that, in a confessional way, she assumes her role in its entirety, from a perspective of a new life. Because it is a discourse in which the first person prevails, it is the "I" itself that emerges, even though it has absorbed traces of its ancestors, what is evident is discourse and individual memory in the present.

Also, making inferences to Benjamin (2012), the narrator character, in narrating her experiences, describes her own life, taking it to the "immeasurable limits of her being" (p.217). (p.217), and this is how Maria Moura fully lives the perplexity of her own being.

> While we were arranging things, it seemed easy, but in reality it was a consummation. I had always lived locked up at home, my sisters-in-law bringing me everything by hand, preparing my bath, washing and ironing my clothes, making special meals because I was a bikini girl. Mum had got me used to it (...). Now that hard life, with only men for company, in that isolated bush, I don't know how I coped. (...). Now I was free of everything, without a home, without an owner, without a family, so what? At least no one would put their foot on my neck; (...) (QUEIROZ, 2000, p. 121122).

We can see, then, that Maria Moura, in narrating her story, shows awareness of the world, her surroundings, longs for change, sparking thoughts that contradict those of her time, most of the time ahead of her time, which leads her to loneliness and, why not say it, suffering;

> We walked a few more kilometres - it was so lonely (...). But with myself, inside my heart and head, nothing was quite right. That for me was just a time of passage or even a beginning, but a small beginning, the first steps on a path that still had to go much, much further. (QUEIROZ, 2000, p. 85, 111-124).

However, as difficult as it may seem, the character doesn't give up on her dreams and sometimes makes the reader wonder about the detachment of being from its bonds. What is it possible to be? In Maria Moura, we have the exasperation of all feelings, whether good or bad, as a mark of protest, pride and hatred, exposing social ills. This exasperation of feelings shows the character's intense truth, her confession of self. As a narrator, Maria Moura establishes an aesthetic reality of the self and the world, informing us of what she deems necessary to consolidate her intentions. The aesthetic effect of the narrative is that of a Truth that could only be apprehended through the perception of a narrator who says that nobody else can speak for her but herself. See SENA (1988),

> But the laws that happen to regulate human relationships are certainly not those of aesthetic creation, even if we admit that everything in the world, even our conception of it, is more of an aesthetic creation than a "truth" that doesn't exist, nor does it really matter if it does. This is so "true" that we could say that our sense of reality is measured by our ability to imagine it (SENA, 1988, p. 12-13).

The assumption of sincerity is aimed at transformation, or rather, it creates the effect of contrast with the reality in which the character is inserted. Maria Moura contradicts common sense and projects an intense and autonomous individuality. When she talks about herself, she becomes self-centred, as if her thoughts were supreme over all others. In her discourse, we find the effect of ambiguity in her accounts, ranging from her clothes to the way she expresses herself. Schpun (2002) argues that, "(...) the masculine clothes she inherited from her father support her reconversion, giving her power and inspiring fear and respect. They do not, however, make her pass for a man". In this respect, for the critic, ambiguity stands out as an element of the character's composition, "all ambiguity lies precisely in the fact that she denies being treated as a "little maid". She claims an identity not as a man, but as a woman of power". (SCHPUN, 2002, p. 183).

> I wouldn't allow people to call me Sinhá, that was a captive thing. But everyone had to call me Dona, or even Dona Moura. I couldn't be just another bacamarte, running the roads in their company, if I didn't even have a firearm with me. I made a point of only carrying my silver-handled dagger on my belt (QUEIROZ, 2000, p. 261).

The boundaries that exist in the narrative of the "I" overlap in form, through the consciousness that it expresses, the rupture of discourse in relation to the social relations of yesteryear. By narrating "from the inside" of the facts, bringing the frustrations, he problematises the human-social concept, giving rise to a constant awareness on an ethical-existential level. The labyrinth of existence and the possible being of each person on an aesthetic level, free and true in the depths of being, the immanence of the self: "If you think he dishonoured me, you're wrong. I was no innocent maiden when Cirino arrived here. I'm a free woman, I give no satisfaction to anyone". (QUEIROZ, 2000, p.450).

The narrator character presents herself with authenticity, letting her words emerge. Word and action, thought and event are the result of a moral awareness of her actions, which are always at stake. What is this supremacy that leads the subject to take precedence over everything and everyone? Wouldn't that be a frivolous optimism that would ultimately make life meaningless? And because she doesn't agree with the thinking of the others she lives with, would it lead Maria Moura to constantly search for new horizons? The immanence of being. We can infer that the discourse used by this narrator borders on the poetic fullness of language in the aesthetic search for truth, for the origin of being, in itself. When we talk about the poetic fullness of the aesthetic for truth, it is because we realise that the discourse she uses starts from personal relationships, from the memories reflected in her memory, which in turn, when enunciated, becomes true through the use of words.

We reiterate that the narrative in **Memorial** de **Maria Moura** shows that in Rachel de Queiroz's works, the characterisation of female characters who do not adhere to marriage or accept social impositions is present. Those who submit to these values, such as Marialva, are in a position to further challenge the ideals of liberation from the role of women in society.

When the persistent search and struggle ceases, Maria Moura bursts into passion for Cirino. Cirino's presence in Serra dos Padres exposes Maria Moura to a new situation. When the time of guerrilla warfare is over, Maria Moura maintains the Serra dos Padres with the demand for refuges for the wanted and for the pairs.

> Antonio Muxió's group continued to do better than expected. I even regretted having disliked the goat. Together with Roque, he was a devil of a pair. They'd spend a fortnight, three weeks away, and never come back empty-handed. It was either money or jewellery, always more than one weapon. Occasionally they would arrive with a few head of cattle. (QUEIROZ, 2000, p.330).

Maria Moura doesn't play an active role in the pair's activities; she is now a kind of administrator of the order and security of Casa Forte - it's true that Duarte concentrated a large part of the duties. Maria Moura's time is taken up by her strong pulse and her attention to detail, from the kitchen to her work. Taking risks, being part of ambushes, is no longer for her. It is in this situation of balance and calm that Maria Moura is forced to take a break from her warrior self.

The short time of passion is born. Cirino shows himself to be the opposite of the model man that Maria Moura took for herself (her father) when she conquered the land. Neither strong nor courageous, he joins the gallery of "Vadinhos" - the character in **Dona Flor and her two husbands.** A conqueror, opportunist and frivolous, he quickly sees Dona Moura's emotional fragility and his opportunity to attain power. Betrayal is a fact expected by the reader, foretold by Cirino's character. The poignant suffering and the tearing of the chest conform the surrender of a narrator committed by love, by hatred. In this vein, Schpun (2002, p.180) argues that Rachel de Queiroz,

> (...) exquisitely expresses the power relations that link men and women, in all their complexity. It expresses the deep ambiguities surrounding the fissure found by Maria Moura to occupy a space of power, so as not to follow the sad fate that would be reserved for her, that is, to be submissive, marrying was not in her plans.

(SCHPUN, 2002, p.180).

From this perspective, we realise that Maria Moura causes disorder in the social environment, occupying a "space of power" and claiming for herself the right to own her truth, even if this brings her suffering, because she has to take on the task of breaking with the values she is constantly searching for.

> The thoughts gnawed at me, strangled me. I couldn't cry. Imagine the surprise, the hatred in that heart. Hate against me! Even if it was just a flash of lightning, the instant the knife whizzed through the air and pierced his chest until it reached his heart (QUEIROZ, 2000, p.460).

In contexts where she had to choose between "me" or the other, Maria Moura was not mediated by her heart, by solidarity. Reason, even in pain, made her will be carried out: "When it came to doing justice, I trusted in my strength: what had to be done was done. And with such care and luck that everything worked out." (QUEIROZ, 2000, p.466). Again, we draw inferences from Mônica Raisa Schpun (2002) who, in her article *Lé, com, lé, cré com cré?* This confrontation between Moura and Cirino is "full of rawness", lack of compassion and violence.

> Locked in my room, alone, thinking about the harm that Cirino had done to me. Not that I was wrong about him, I know I wasn't. My evil was that great weakness I felt for him. I liked to call it love. But only because I thought it was beautiful and because, in love, everything is forgiven. But it wasn't love, it was worse (...). And now I - I had to face that betrayal. Not of love, which can be forgiven, but of faith. Betrayal of Maria Moura, the woman Cirino boasted about in the girls' house, who ate out of the palm of his hand (...). Who else was going to take Maria Moura at her word? To this day, Moura had never made a false statement to anyone. An enemy is an enemy, but a partner and a friend is a very different definition (QUEIROZ, 2000, p.418).

In her solitude, Maria Moura confesses all her anguish over her betrayal and her decision to kill Cirino. In her confessional speech, she confronts the inequality between the role of men and women in society, with underlying revelations that make us reflect on the negative nature of this society, which, impregnated with prejudice, destroys the human being. It is in this sense that the character loves herself, in order to preserve herself and be alive for the events. In Maria Moura we see lyricism marked by a memory in solitude. She is a lonely character who constantly needs to restore her past in order to find herself again. We can see that the rupture in Maria Moura materialises in her relationship with society; her "I" does not consent to inequality and submission. It was not by chance that, on leaving her native home, she took possession of the inheritance left to her by her father: the trousers and the belt. He became a man and took up his goal of fighting for the lands dreamt of by his grandfather and then by his father. We realise, then, that Maria Moura's confessional speech is proof of what Bakhtin (2010) says, that the person who speaks in the novel always represents a particular point of view on the world. And because she aspires to this idea of liberation, Maria Moura narrates as if she were starting all over again:

> _ Sinhá Dona, it looks like we're going to fight with the king's soldiers! And I smiled: "Who knows? (...). And if I was preparing the men, I also took care of myself; I sorted out my rifle, had João Rufo oil it, cleaned any rust spots and prepared the ammunition. I even took care of my clothes: just one change. I wasn't going to take a hammock, nor was anyone else. On a campaign trip, you walk lightly. I had some old, loose boots polished for my comfort. And I was going to inaugurate my leather gibbon, well stitched; often, Roque said, it's used to deflect lead that comes from behind or skewed. Everything was just right, as the boys used to say. In fact, I was preparing myself and my men for that raid like I was preparing for a party (QUEIROZ, 2000, p.476).

Always placed in a position of confrontation, her calculated attitudes reflect the fate of fulfilling a duty. Dialoguing with the force of tradition, the transgression of the woman who invades the male world leads to a reflection on established and consecrated power. Presented as the force of her own desire, she sees herself in her father's image: "- I know I'm different. But as I told you, I only hurt those who hurt me first" (QUEIROZ, 2000, p.380). This belief in strength, which appears to be inherent in her, will guide her towards the security of action, revenge and conquest. Maria Moura has an essence of truth within her, through her own life story, the memory that underlies the understanding of her entire discourse, in an individual existence.

The Confession of the "I" brings recognition for having acted against the principles in force, as he states in his memoirs. This recognition empties itself of guilt and absorbs the sacredness of life and sincerity in what he believes to be true.

FINAL CONSIDERATIONS

The process of configuring memory and confession allows social and historical issues to be problematised based on the condition of women in the backlands. The memorial discourse intends to reorder a world seen from Maria Moura's perspective.

In the first chapter, we study some of the female characters in four novels and one stage text, with the aim of getting to know the literary system produced by Rachel de Queiroz. And to understand how her production was situated in the early years of the 20th century. Along the way, we identified how certain discursive elements recur in the configuration of both the narrator and the protagonist character. From this primary survey, we came to the conclusion of a recurrence of memory as a formal aspect of her novels, above all, considering the breakdown of the family, based on the construction of antagonistic relationships in the female universe, in contexts of patriarchal structure, in the Brazilian sertão. They are poignant narratives because they deal with violence in its various forms. This does not mean that they are pessimistic narratives. Rachel de Queiroz's literary system has a thematic and formal unity, an aesthetic coherence. We could say that it pursues a cause, whose protagonists are committed to defending it. The values of her time are more than explicit in them. The existential problem is realised by the conflict between generations, between classes, between genders, with the patriarchal rural world as its absolute context. From **O Quinze** (1930) to **Dôra Doralina** (1975), the strength of writing about the condition of women in the sertão was consolidated. Dôra's transformation is noticeable through her wandering life in the theatre company, her desire for freedom and her profession as an actress. In the meantime, Dôra returns to her native home, back to living with the forms of the past, occupying the place left by her mother. Her trajectory largely reproduces her mother's life story, albeit in a perpetual act of denial. In this process of configuration, both characters break the reader's expectations and announce memory as a way of understanding and reading themselves, in the search for a fragmented totality of being. **Beata Maria do Egito** (1958) is no different. The woman appears as an instrument of faith and the struggle for an ideology of life in search of her space, which in turn fragments the being in its individuality. The character Beata's drama is explicit, her suffering in the search for the truth she believes in. A religious cause that is permeated by fanaticism, which causes her soul to ache as she gives in to the whims of others. In her discourse, the fictional and literary reality is of a visual world strongly marked by immanent force, present in the female character in a scenario in which we contemplate antagonistic forces. In **Memorial de Maria Moura** (1992), Marialva's narrative reinforces the maintenance of a woman's existence exclusively through marriage, motherhood and submission.

In the second chapter, we turn to the corpus of our research. We discuss the configuration of memory in the discourse of the character Maria Moura. The discourse of the past, in the present, through memories, reordered into an identity of the "I". The fabric of memory gives rise to the narrative as a mirror of the "I". In this, the scope of an entire life extends from childhood to old age. In Maria Moura, the memorial discourse, on the level of enunciation, establishes a relationship between the self and the world, far beyond what was lived, the aesthetics of confession seeks to grasp the true meaning and emotion, retained as a perception of the "self". The dynamics that the narrator uses to tell her memories, the events, generate a rupture in relation to the society to which she belongs. Her memoiristic discourse creates a panel of the patriarchal system, at the same time as reflecting on centuries-old forms of repression and violence. In this chapter, we come close to a narrator and a character who have been humanised by their error and courage in assuming power, thereby causing disorder in society because they are female narrators and characters.

In the third chapter, we look at confession as a discursive way of saying "I". Apologetically, confession recovers the aesthetic effect of sincerity and truth. We briefly look at Rousseau in **Confessions.** We bring the understanding postulated by Rousseau to bear on Maria Moura's confession. The aesthetic effect of her discourse advocates self-centredness, launching the character (and also the novel) into a distant tradition of "writing of the self", from autobiography to the autobiographical novel. This type of writing leads to the character's affective fragility, the mark of an individuality, of a being in the world, unique and irrepressible. The consistency of this individuality is moulded by contradictions, mistakes and imperfections. From this discourse of the "I", confession is the ritualisation of an act and the immanence of being. Maria Moura has developed an individualistic discourse based on the sensibility effect of "me" and the "I".

other. Her actions oppose patriarchal society. In a constant struggle with herself and the space she inhabits (social, political), her word, like an ideologeme, transfigures reality. Her word, sometimes authoritarian, organised from a hierarchical past, does not cancel out the persuasive word. In the character, the persuasive word is coherent, since it is configured in the relationship of communication with the other, with the other characters (Duarte, Marialva, João Rufo, etc), using negotiation, according to the interests of the present. This observation of the word, in these two horizons of realisation (authoritative and persuasive), does not allow the narrative of Maria Moura's memoirs to escape a considerable degree of objectification. This objectification always puts a boundary between "I" and the other in crisis. There is a process of struggle, of the word, on the level of memory, to signify an individual and historical consciousness. As if the "I" were saying: "I have the word now". But the word escapes its influence alone, and says something about the other, taking on a complex meaning because it is born of others (like the Father and the Grandfather), in an ideologically determined context.

Maria Moura's memories carry traces of ancestry (from her father to her grandfather), in a timeline that refers to other times, beyond her own. This dialogical relationship of discourse in the novel reveals the transmission and representation of tradition and culture. In the trajectory of a character, we have ways of interpreting culture in the specific universe of artistic representation in the novel.

BIBLIOGRAPHY

AUTHIER-REVUZ, J. **Between transparency and opacity:** an enunciative study of meaning. Porto Alegre: EDIPUCRS, 2004.

BACHELARD, Gaston. **The dialectic of duration.** São Paulo: Ática, 1994.

The Poetics of Space. São Paulo: Martins Fontes, 2000.

BAKHTIN, Mikhail. **Aesthetics of Verbal Creation;** introduction and translation from the Russian Paulo Bezerra; preface to the French edition Tzvetan.-4ª Ed. São Paulo: Martins Fontes,2003. 2ª edition 2006.

 Questions of Literature and Aesthetics (The Theory of the Novel). 6ª Ed. São Paulo: Hucitec, 2010.

Problems of Dostoiewski's Poetics. 3ª ed. Rio de Janeiro: Forense Universitária, 2005.

BENJAMIN, Walter. **The** Narrator. In: **Magic and technique, art and politics: essays on literature and cultural history.** São Paulo: Brasiliense, 2012 (Selected works v. 1).

BERGSON, H. **Matter and Memory.** São Paulo: Perspectiva, 2011 .

BLANCHOT, Maurice. **The book to come.** Translation: Leyla Perrone-Moisés. São Paulo: Martins Fontes, 2005.

BOSI, Alfredo. **Concise History of Brazilian Literature.** 44 ed. Cultrix. São Paulo, 2006.

CÂNDIDO, Antonio. **Literature and society.** 11ª ed. Rio de Janeiro: Ouro sobre Azul,2010.

CHEVALIER, J. GHEERBRANT, A. **Dictionary of Symbols.** Rio de Janeiro: José Olympio, 1998.

COELHO. Nelly Novais. **Critical dictionary of Brazilian women writers.** São Paulo: Escrituras Editora, 2002.

COSTA, Lima. **Literature and the reader.** 2ª ed. Rio de Janeiro: Paz e Terra, 2011.

COURTEAU, Joanna. The feminisation of national discourse in the work of Rachel de Queiroz. In: **A jounal devoted to the teaching of Spanish in Portuguese, published by the American Association of Teachers of Spanish and Portuguese, Inc.** Vol.84. Number 4.December 2001.

ECO, Umberto. **Interpretation and Superinterpretation.** São Paulo: Martins Fontes, 2005.

FRANCESCHI, Antonio Fernando. **Brazilian Literature Notebooks.** Number *4.* São Paulo: IMS, 1997.

GALVÃO, Walnice Nogueira. **A Donzela-Guerreira - A study of the genre.** São Paulo: Ed.SENAC, 1998.

HALBWACHS, Maurice. **Collective Memory.** 2ª Ed. São Paulo: Centauro, 2006.

HALL, S. **A identidade cultural na Pós-modernidade,** 11ª Ed. Rio de Janeiro: DP&A, 2011.

_____. Who needs identity? In: **Identidade e diferença: A perspectiva dos estudos culturais/** Tomaz Tadeu da Silva (org.) Petrópolis- Rio de Janeiro: Vozes, 2002.

HOLLANDA, Heloisa Buarque de.(Org.) **Tendências e Impasses. Feminism as a critique of culture.** Rio de Janeiro: Rocco, 1994.

http://www.bibliotecadigital.ufmg.br/dspace/handle/1843/ECAP-8H5PXP 02/04/2013. 02/04/2013. 15:07
http://www.sapientia.pucsp.br/tde_search/file.php?codFile=11134 18/09/2013. 17:35

http://www.heloisabuarquedehollanda.com.br/o-ethos-rachel/ 13/11/2013. 16:44

KAYSER, Wolfgang. **Analysing and interpreting literary works.** 6ª edition. São Paulo: Martins Fontes, 1976.

KUNDERA, Milan. **The art of the novel.** São Paulo: Companhia das Letras, 2009.

MACHADO, Irene. **The novel and the voice.** Mikhail Bakhtin's prosaic dialogue. Rio de Janeiro: Imago/FAPESP, 1995.

QUEIROZ, Rachel de. **The Fifteen.** São Paulo: José Olympio, 1930.

Dôra, Doralina. 20ª Ed. Rio de Janeiro: José Olympio, 2004.

The Blessed Maria of Egypt. 5ª ed. Rio de Janeiro: José Olympio, 2005.

Memorial de Maria Moura. 12ª Ed. São Paulo: Siciliano, 2000.

QUEIROZ, Rachel de. QUEIROZ, Maria Luiza de. **Tantos anos.** 4ª ed. São Paulo: ARX, 2004.

QUEIROZ, Rachel de. **Coleção Melhores Crônicas.** Selection and Foreword by Heloísa Buarque de Hollanda. São Paulo: Global, 2004.

REIS, Carlos; LOPES, Ana Cristina M. **Dicionário de teoria da narrativa.** São Paulo. Ática, 1988.

ROSSI, Paolo. **The past, memory, forgetting.** São Paulo: Ed. UNESP, 2010.

ROUSSEAU, Jean-Jacques. **Confessions.** São Paulo: Edipro, 2008.

SENA, Jorge de. Rousseau's "Confessions" and the problem of sincerity. Preface. In: **Confessions.** ROUSSEAU, Jean-Jacques. Translated by Fernando Lopes Graça. Volume I. Lisbon. Relógio d'Água, 1998.

SCHPUN, M.R. **Lé com lé, crê com crê.** In: Literature and culture in Brazil: identities and frontiers/ CHIAPPINI, L.BRESCIANI, M. S. (eds.). - São Paulo: Cortez, 2002.

SILVA, Vitor de Aguiar e. **Theory of Literature.** 8ª ed. Coimbra: Edições Almedina, 2007.

TACCA, Oscar. **The voices of the novel.** Coimbra - Portugal: Livraria Almedina, 1983.

TODOROV, Tzvetan. **Poetics of Prose.** São Paulo: Martins Fontes, 2003.

VILALVA, Walnice. The narrative pact in Memorial de Maria Moura. In: **Um pouco acima do chão: entre ciência e arte.** VILALVA, Walnice (Org.). Tangará da Serra: Editora Diário da Serra, 2012.

WEISCHEDEL, Wilhelm. **Roussesu or The Unfortunate Sentimental Thinker.** In: The Back Stairs of Philosophy. Translated by Edson Dognaldo Gil. São Paulo: Angra, 1999.

I want morebooks!

Buy your books fast and straightforward online - at one of world's fastest growing online book stores! Environmentally sound due to Print-on-Demand technologies.

Buy your books online at
www.morebooks.shop

Kaufen Sie Ihre Bücher schnell und unkompliziert online - auf einer der am schnellsten wachsenden Buchhandelsplattformen weltweit! Dank Print-On-Demand umwelt- und ressourcenschonend produziert.

Bücher schneller online kaufen
www.morebooks.shop

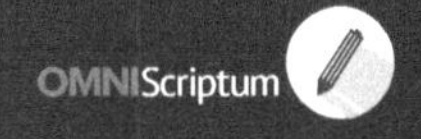

Printed by Books on Demand GmbH, Norderstedt / Germany